THE MEADOW AT
CHAPEL HILL CROSS

THE MEADOW AT CHAPEL HILL CROSS

ROGER MANN

Copyright © 2022 Roger Mann

The moral right of the author has been asserted.

Apart from any fair dealing for the purposes of research or private study, or criticism or review, as permitted under the Copyright, Designs and Patents Act 1988, this publication may only be reproduced, stored or transmitted, in any form or by any means, with the prior permission in writing of the publishers, or in the case of reprographic reproduction in accordance with the terms of licences issued by the Copyright Licensing Agency. Enquiries concerning reproduction outside those terms should be sent to the publishers.

Matador
Unit E2 Airfield Business Park,
Harrison Road, Market Harborough,
Leicestershire. LE16 7UL
Tel: 0116 2792299
Email: books@troubador.co.uk
Web: www.troubador.co.uk/matador
Twitter: @matadorbooks

ISBN 978 1803131 757

British Library Cataloguing in Publication Data.
A catalogue record for this book is available from the British Library.

Printed and bound in the UK by TJ Books Ltd, Padstow, Cornwall
Typeset in 11pt Adobe Garamond Pro by Troubador Publishing Ltd, Leicester, UK

Matador is an imprint of Troubador Publishing Ltd

"Even as we pitch our wicket, flickering near are shades of men who found this cricket dear and sealed their happy ventures ere we came."

Thomas Moult

CHAPTER ONE

In the old days, Saturdays were special!

How I missed that magic moment when it was time to pack my cricket bag!

First my boots, with their studs still encased by dried mud, followed by a hastily folded shirt, and then a pair of whites with a grass-stained knee.

These days, Saturday afternoons had become just a series of television programmes!

The punishment for growing old was a choice between horse racing and Formula One, interspersed by adverts for life insurance and stair-lifts.

But, just for today, I had decided to change all that!!!

The sun was shining, and I was going to stroll down the road to spend an hour watching Barton play in a Devon League match. A peck on the cheek for Jenny, a cheery "I won't be long, darling!" and I was on my way.

As I approached the ground, it struck me how little had changed since I first played here, sixty-five years ago. The stone pavilion, with its red tiled roof, was beginning to look tired. The giant oak tree had gone, but otherwise I might have stepped back into the 1950s.

The match had already started, so I waited for the end of an over, then tiptoed behind the spectators towards a vacant deckchair.

It was up in the corner, near to the top hedge. Nice and private... Perfect! I could watch the play from here, and maybe even have a quick doze in the sunshine.

It was good to be back at the old ground after so long!

A tall, thin boy was batting, and the scoreboard showed that he was on 24 not out.

He looked so pale and young as he played a precise little shot down to third man, and ran a single. The man in front of me exchanged a smile with his wife, and applauded politely.

Pale, precise, and polite were not epithets which would have described cricket at Barton in my day!!

After a while, I closed my eyes, and somewhere deep inside my head I could hear Dave Morgan offering mild insults from behind the stumps.

Then I was facing another over from Bill Cassells. Six balls out of six, right on the same spot, and I was playing back another maiden!

"Well bowled, Bill," I whispered, as his follow-through left him inches from my face. He turned away without acknowledgement. This was Barton, and I was Torquay!

I shifted in my deckchair, and, next, I was running in to bowl to a smiling Roy Horswell. Even now, I could feel the pain in the pit of my stomach as he drove my first ball, all along the ground, to the long-off boundary.

The figures were growing dim now, but I could still make out Bill Parsons fielding at mid-off, and a cheery Ted Davenport walking back to his bowling mark.

I glanced up to the pavilion, and, there, under the oak tree, George Stuckey was parking his taxi.

Then it all grew dark, my head dropped, and I felt utterly relaxed… until I was woken by a sharp dig in the ribs!

CHAPTER TWO

"Out of my way, dear! How can I sweep the floor with you day-dreaming there?"

Molly, my wife, was a good woman and kept our little house in Devonport like, as she would often say, "a brass button". There was not room enough for Molly, the broom, and me, so I stood up, smiled, and stepped out into the porch.

Perhaps a walk was just what I needed to stop me thinking about tomorrow. I laced my boots, and stepped out on to St. Aubyn Street.

It was a sunny Sunday morning, in 1853, and the warm air refreshed me.

As I reached George Street, the traffic became heavier.

Carts clattered along the cobbles, all heading for the dockyard.

Twice I felt the rump of a horse brush my elbow, and ease me towards the gutter.

It was a relief to leave the main road, to reach the lines (our name for the wall of the garrison), and to find a quiet spot overlooking the water.

I leaned back against the stone wall, unlaced my boots, and, at last, had time to think.

This time tomorrow, I would be umpiring the All England Eleven! Yes! Me!

The most important match in the whole of England would be staged in Torquay on Monday, 22nd August 1853, and I would play a major part in it!

OK! The United England Eleven were playing at Bradford, but they were just upstarts by comparison to the A.E.E.

As I thought about it, I felt myself taking deep breaths, and realised that I was smiling.

My mind raced back to the early days when I used to umpire in scratch matches on Devonport Hill. No one bothered with the rules in those days, until I came along!

But no! It really all began twelve years ago, in 1841, when the Commander-In-Chief of the British Army decreed that every garrison in England should provide a cricket ground.

At the time, I was a part-time painter working at Devonport dockyard.

Cricket was the last thing on my mind when, one morning, I noticed an advert posted on the gates of the Plymouth Garrison.

It said that a painter was required for some piece-work in the barracks.

Anyone interested should see the garrison secretary, Captain Rush of the 77th regiment.

I reported to the gate that same afternoon, and was taken in to see him.

Because I was a painter by trade, he knew that I could do the work, but not just any old tradesman was allowed to operate within the garrison walls.

"What do you favour doing in your off time?" he asked.

"Cricket sir! And I love every breath of it!" I replied.

He got up, smiled, and said, "As do I." We shook hands and my life changed from that day.

Afterwards, whenever I was painting in the barracks, the captain would search me out and we would exchange views on the latest scores in *Bell's Life*. We became firm friends.

Early in 1843, the garrison got its cricket ground, and, by the summer, it was in regular use. Captain Rush and I took our turns to umpire internal matches, and a groundsman was hired to use the garrison's new Budding's mower and its wide range of scythes.

In years gone by, the officers of the garrison had played their matches at Mount Edgcumbe, but now they could offer opponents the hospitality of their own private ground.

Obviously, it would be some while before I was invited to umpire in the garrison's club matches, but I watched the games against visiting teams like Sidmouth and North Devon, and made sure that I learned from every one of them.

In June 1845, as a registered M.C.C. umpire, I received notification from the Marylebone Club that there had been some minor revisions to the Laws of Cricket.

I applied for a poster version of the revised laws, and displayed it in the garrison's pavilion.

This seemed to raise my status with the officers, and, in August, I was invited to officiate in a match against the Lansdowne Club from Bath. I was soon regarded as a senior umpire.

During 1846, I was often needed at the dockyard, so that summer, my cricket took a back seat.

However, Captain Rush was patient with me, and on 1st July 1847 he asked me to travel with the garrison to my most important appointment yet… to Teignbridge Cricket Club, near Newton Abbot.

Throughout the county, Teignbridge was the most highly respected club of all, and I remember buying a new frock coat for the occasion.

CHAPTER THREE

The Teignbridge ground was less than two miles from the town of Newton Abbot, and my first sight of it took my breath away.

It was absolutely flat with a thatched pavilion and a spacious marquee, all overlooked by the Dartmoor hills behind it. How I would love to umpire here every week!

The coach stopped at the gate and, as the officers filed into the pavilion, I made my way out towards the mown area of the ground where a man was stamping on the turf.

As I got closer, I could see that today's pitch had been selected, and that the creases had already been painted. This had never happened to me before!

Everyone knew that the visiting team's captain chose where the pitch would be positioned, and that the visitors' umpire then cut the creases with his knife... even at Teignbridge!

Fred Bell, the Teignbridge umpire, stopped stamping and walked over towards me.

"Saved you the trouble us did," he said. "I knows her well, and she'll be a booty." As he spoke, it was clear to me that new turfs had been laid recently, and that they were not settling in well.

Fred had been trying to stamp them down, but some corners were rising already, and new grass had not yet hidden the divisions between them.

However, it was too late to change things now, so I accompanied Fred back to the umpires' room at the back of the pavilion.

The match was due to begin at midday, but it wasn't until after the last two Teignbridge players had arrived on horseback at about 12.20 that we walked out to the middle.

After losing a wicket in the first over, Teignbridge began to build its innings slowly.

Then at 1.30 a bell rang and the two batsmen nodded to each other, and headed off towards the pavilion, beckoning the rest of us to follow.

The over was incomplete, and I had been given no indication that a break would be taken!

Fred told me to hold my tongue and to follow him, because platters of bread and cheese had been laid out in the pavilion, and flagons of cider would be lined up behind them.

The players were meeting for the first time, so made the best of this unexpected hospitality.

Naturally, umpires were not allowed into the pavilion, so I settled down on a bench and was quite pleased when we were able to get the match underway again at 2.00.

No further wickets fell before a second bell was rung at 3.45. Now it was time for lunch!

This time, at least, the batsmen waited until the over was completed before leaving the field!

Fred and I followed the players off and he went over to chat with the scorers, whilst I got the chance to peep through the main door of the pavilion, and to watch the merriment with my own eyes.

It was dark inside, but full of laughter and bonhomie. The players would soon be consuming some thick cuts of meat, laid out in front of flagons of cider.

I had just gone back to my seat on the bench, under the eaves of the pavilion, when Fred walked over towards me carrying two porcelain bowls.

"'Tis a tradition for us 'ere at Teignbridge. 'Ave some," he said and handed me a bowl filled to the brim with cold plum pudding, soaked in a "Teignbridge" sauce.

Making vigorous stirring motions with his right hand, he explained that Teignbridge sauce was made from Devonshire cream beaten up with brandy. I didn't need a second invitation!

At about 4.30, Fred and I walked out to the middle, and we were followed by the officers.

Some minutes later, the two batsmen left the pavilion talking together loudly, and by the time they reached the pitch they were roaring with laughter.

Mr. Harris, who had opened the batting, prepared to face the bowling of Captain Budd.

Before doing so, he smiled at me and said, "Be kind to me umpire sir!" and belched loudly.

The first ball was a wide, but, soon after that, the cider began to play its tricks, and wickets started to tumble. Mr. Harris was dismissed, and others shared the same fate.

Mr. Taylor, batting at number six for the hosts, was soon required.

He was a short, stout man, and, with his billycock cap pulled down over his eyes, he followed a winding path to the wicket. He took a huge swing at the first ball, and spun around in a circle as it tipped the edge of his bat and went down to long stop for a single.

When it was time to face his next ball, he tried the same again, but, this time, he missed it completely, and fell on to the stumps! It took a full minute to persuade him that he was out!

As the Teignbridge innings was drawing to a close, some of the non-playing members of the club had arrived to play bowls on the outfield. Pretty soon, some began shouting as the fielders chased the ball amongst them, just as they were measuring from the jack.

As luck would have it, the hosts were bowled out soon after 6.30, for 164, so we were able to bring the day's play to an end, before feelings boiled over.

I said goodbye to Fred as the players filed back into the pavilion.

Over beside the river bank, the coachman was backing the horses between the shafts of the garrison's coach.

I strolled over, and he told me that we would be staying at the Globe Hotel in Newton Abbot tonight, and that he expected to make the journey many times before the night was over!

"They'll be drinking their 'ealth 'til midnight, and there's many amongst them officers who'll end up very 'ealthy I'll be bound!"

An hour later, three of the younger officers had joined us and the coachman climbed up into the box seat to take us the two miles back to the hotel.

The centre of Newton Abbot was crowded this evening, and carriages were queuing up outside the hotel.

I climbed out of the coach, thanked the coachman, and felt a tug on my arm. "A blessing to you sir!" said the old gypsy woman, holding out a skinny hand towards me.

I forced a smile. "And to you, my dear," I replied, as I pushed my way towards the brightly lit entrance. I followed the three young officers into one of the coffee rooms, but a thick cloud of tobacco smoke soon made me change my mind.

As an umpire, I felt more comfortable eating on my own, so, instead, I made my way into the supper room, which was almost empty. I ordered a sandwich from the hotel's "Arrangement of Carte", and reflected on the decisions I had made during the day.

I had been upset that the pitch had been chosen and cut without my supervision, but in the end Fred's stamping had cured most of its faults, and, overall, the cricket had not been compromised.

It had been a long, exciting day, and I would sleep well tonight.

*

The following morning was a Friday, and the garrison team's breakfast was served in the Assembly Room.

Although I had eaten by nine o'clock, it was clear that most of the team had not yet stirred. Slowly, one by one, four more bleary-eyed officers made their way down the stairs, and joined us at the long trestle table.

Stories of a riotous night began to circulate, and it was clear that the Teignbridge hospitality had lived up to its reputation.

At 10.30, the coachman sent word to say that the horses had left the stabling, and were ready to leave, as arranged, but no one seemed to take any notice.

A further forty minutes passed before Captain Budd had finally gathered his team together in front of the hotel, and watched them board the coach.

I felt guilty that I was going to be too late to supervise the groundsman, but assumed Fred's stamping would once again give us a playable surface for the garrison innings… but how wrong I turned out to be!

A shout from the coachman released the horses. There was a jolt, and we were on our way.

As soon as we arrived at the ground, I walked out towards the middle. From a distance, I could see that the new turfs had risen overnight, and that neither Fred nor the groundsman were anywhere to be seen!

When I got to the pitch, I was horrified to see that its surface had been pitted with dozens of deep hoof marks!

I found Fred in the umpires' room, and asked him what had happened.

"I'm thinking 'tis the South Devon Hunt that crossed it!" he said.

I told him that I wouldn't allow the match to start before something was done about it, and asked him to call for the groundsman.

"He's been gone for an hour now," was his response.

This time, I was not going to be ignored, and told him that he should have taken some action.

He sat there and stared blankly as I walked out, and slammed the door.

Knowing an umpire would not be welcomed inside, I walked around to the main door of the pavilion and asked to see the two captains outside.

I sensed that Captain Budd and the Teignbridge captain, Mr. Sanders, were a little surprised to be summoned, and both appeared impatient. "Whatever's this about?" asked Mr. Sanders.

I explained that the pitch was no longer fit to bat on, and that I wanted all twenty-two players to come out and stamp it down before I would allow play to commence!

THE MEADOW AT CHAPEL HILL CROSS

After the stamping, I demanded that table tops, from the marquee, be removed from their trestles, and upturned. Then, each top was to be stood upon by four men, and pressed down upon the playing surface until any remaining ridges were flattened.

Finally, I needed to see that the pitch was swept of all the resulting debris.

Perhaps because it was their turn to bat, the officers were first to set about the task.

The Teignbridge team showed far less enthusiasm, but, one by one, strolled out to help.

By 12.30, the surface was looking better, although a number of the ridges had resisted all attempts to flatten them.

A small crowd had gathered over by the river, and I was able to tell the teams that play would begin in fifteen minutes.

Captain Budd opened the garrison's innings with Lt. Johnson, and, at first, the pitch played well.

However, after ten overs, the bowler's follow-through began to loosen one of the turfs at the pavilion end, leaving a deep crevice just outside the leg stump. It looked ominous!

When 1.30 came, I made certain this time that I personally announced the bread and cheese break, and that the over was properly completed.

When play resumed after the break, Mr. Sanders soon noticed the crevice, and threw the ball to Mr. Bere, his heavily muscled fast bowler. Mr. Bere had a short run, but delivered from very wide of the stumps... just right to find the crevice.

His second ball hit the top of Captain Budd's off-stump, and the garrison's innings began to collapse. Mr. Sanders's lobs accounted for Lt. Johnson, and Captain Muster managed to run a four before becoming Mr. Bere's next victim.

When the innings closed, Mr. Bere had taken eight wickets. All were clean bowled, and most had hit the crevice, and gone on to hit the bottom of the off stump.

The innings closed on 64, exactly 100 runs short of the Teignbridge score. Lunch followed and no one seemed unduly upset by the pitch, nor by the score.

All that mattered was that the meat was plentiful, and that the flagons of cider were renewed regularly. Fred had disappeared into the umpire's room without a word.

I missed his company almost as much as the cold plum pudding which we had enjoyed together yesterday.

A young girl, no more than twelve years old, was sent out with two tongue sandwiches. One for me, and one for the coachman, so I strolled over to the river to deliver it to him.

When play restarted, with no chance of winning the match before dark, the garrison team decided to throw caution to the wind and to go for broke.

Mr. Sanders brought on his occasional bowlers, and the batsmen hit hard at every ball.

All eyes were now on an early finish, and the ladies' night which was to follow it.

Predictably, seven of the garrison batsmen were caught, and, in less than an hour, the team was dismissed for just 23 runs.

At the end, the players left the field with an almost indecent haste.

I was tired now, and found the same bench, under the eaves of the pavilion, which I had used yesterday.

In my heart I knew that there would be very few young officers who would want to leave a ladies' night early, so I reconciled myself to a long evening staring up at the stars!

However, just as I was feeling sorry for myself, I heard the pounding of hooves from near to the gateway to the ground. I looked up, and saw a horseman galloping towards me.

A shout of "Whoa!" brought the horse skidding to a halt in front of me, and a tall man in his twenties leapt from the saddle. "Prithee sir! Take my hand!" he said, reaching out towards me.

We shook hands, and he wrapped the reins of his horse around one of the posts of the pavilion balcony.

Smiling broadly, he sat down on the bench beside me and introduced himself as John Yarde-Buller from the nearby coastal town of Paignton.

He had been watching the game until lunchtime, and had been deeply impressed by my insistence that the pitch be stamped before play began.

"It was a proper pleasure to see you there, in a smart frock coat, directing those gentlemen to defer to the laws of the game!" he said. "Cricket needs more of the likes of you, sir!"

Before long, it was clear that he loved cricket as much as I did, and was enjoying my company. He told me about his younger days at Eton and Oxford University, and how he had missed out on winning a blue through illness.

He had wanted to join the military, but had got married two years ago instead. His wife would be arriving by carriage soon, and she never missed one of the ladies' nights. Although he was not yet a member of Teignbridge Cricket Club, he would be joining next year, and was looking forward to the chance to do so.

It was a long journey from Paignton, but there were no other cricket clubs which were "fit for gentlemen" any closer to home. Most of the Teignbridge players came from more distant

Teignbridge Cricket Ground – A Painting by Nicholas Felix in 1851

THE MEADOW AT CHAPEL HILL CROSS

TEIGNBRIDGE. July 1st & 2nd, 1847. PLYMOUTH GARRISON.

	1st Innings.		2nd Innings.			1st Innings.		2nd Innings.	
G. Harris	39	b Master	......	Capt. Budd	10	b Bere	2	c Kitson.
Calmady	0	b Townsend	......	Johnson	17	b Sanders	4	c Davis.
C. Lloyd	44	b Budd	......	Muster	4	b Bere	4	b Bere.
J. Divett	5	b Master	......	Lousada	0	b Bere	2	c Harris.
E. Sanders	3	b Townsend	......	Townsend	0	b Bere	1	c Calmady.
H. Taylor	1	h.w.	......	Jones	0	b Bere	0	c Sanders.
J. Kitson	16	c Master	......	Horne	3	c Lloyd	3	run out.
M. Bere	10	b Townsend	......	A. Master	0	b Bere	0	c Lloyd.
E. Seale	0	b Townsend	......	Knapp	2	not out		not out.
J. M. Davis	18	not out	......	Dodsworthy	3	b Bere	0	c Lloyd.
H. Studdy	10	b Master	......	Trevor	10	b Bere	3	b Bere.
Extras	17			Extras	15		4	
	164				64		23	

Teignbridge won by 1 innings and 77 runs.

Teignbridge C.C. v. Plymouth Garrison at Teignbridge in 1847

parishes anyway, and all those whom he had met considered the club's renowned hospitality well worth the effort!

By now, the music of the Amadora Waltz was filling the air, and it wasn't long before a carriage pulled up outside the pavilion.

Mr. John leapt forward, opened the carriage door, and offered his hand to support his wife as she slowly emerged into the evening air.

Charlotte was wearing a dome-shaped, voluminous skirt, and was trying hard to keep it out of the mud which had formed around the pavilion entrance.

In moments, other couples had come out to greet them, and I became just one in a crowd.

As they entered the pavilion, Mr. John turned around, searched to find me, and waved goodbye. I knew, at that moment, that I had made a good friend.

Fred had long gone, so I spent the next two hours chatting with the coachman whilst he washed down his vehicle in the semi-dark.

At around ten o'clock, the officers began to emerge from the pavilion and make their way towards the coach for the journey home. Some arm in arm, and others shouting goodbyes to newfound friends.

Captain Budd had offered to give two of the Teignbridge players a lift home, so I climbed up to the driver's bench seat. The coach jerked forward, and then tilted this way and that as it made its way across the grass towards the main road.

I got home in the early hours of the next morning knowing that, during the last two days, I had at last become the sort of umpire I had always wanted to be.

CHAPTER FOUR

Later in the season, Teignbridge visited the garrison for the return match, and I agreed to umpire once again.

This time, Teignbridge fielded a much weaker team, and, although Mr. Bere took five of the garrison's wickets, we ended up winning by an innings and three runs.

During the next few years, painting took more and more of my time, and I restricted myself to umpiring only inter-garrison matches. Although Captain Rush offered me the chance to travel to other two-day matches, I turned him down, politely. The extra money would have been useful, but sitting outside pavilions for hours, whilst others celebrated, could be quite a lonely experience for the away team's umpire.

By 1849, a lot of cricket clubs began to acquire light rollers, and in the same year the M.C.C. announced a new law allowing pitches to be rolled and swept between innings.

Permission would be granted, subject to a request to the umpires being made within one minute of an innings closing.

The old method of stamping would now be unnecessary, and, of course, my mind went rushing back to my experience at Teignbridge two years earlier.

In the autumn of 1850, Captain Rush called me into his office and told me that John Yarde-Buller had been appointed as the new secretary of Teignbridge Cricket Club for the 1851 season. He had heard me talk of Mr. John, and thought I would be pleased to hear the news.

I was delighted, of course, and wrote to my new friend that same evening.

He responded promptly, and at length.

He had so many plans of how to improve the club, but told me that the turfs had never fully settled down, and, as a result, the pitch was playing worse than ever now.

He ended by saying that, if the money could be raised, his dream would be to invite the All England Eleven to play at Teignbridge in 1851! What an event that would be!!

As it turned out, Mr. John's dreams were answered, and, on 29th September 1851, the great All England Eleven set foot in Devon for the very first time, and headed for Teignbridge.

Their match, against 22 of Devonshire, attracted huge crowds, and, of course, provided a perfect excuse for celebration.

A sumptuous supper in honour of the Eleven was held in the marquee on the first night, and on the following evening one of the newspapers recalled that,

"A splendid ball took place at the Globe Hotel, at which many families of distinction were present. There was a large amount of beauty and fashion, and dancing was kept up until daylight did appear."

Bell's Life reported that Fred Bell had been one of the umpires, and how I envied him!!

During the winter months, most of my work was provided by the dockyard, and the winter of 1851/52 was no exception.

THE MEADOW AT CHAPEL HILL CROSS

In April of 1852, I read that Teignbridge Cricket Club had arranged a second match against the All England Eleven to be played in late August.

Perhaps I would be able to travel there to watch it… or, maybe that was a dream too far!

As always, I had made myself available to umpire the inter-garrison matches, but the fine weather meant that painting, at the dockyard, kept me busy.

Several of the junior officers had asked me to train them to become umpires, and they stepped in for me when I was needed at work.

Then, one day towards the end of July, Captain Rush asked me to come to his office.

He gave me a seat, and then told me that he had had a surprise visit from a Mr. Stockdale, who was a committee member of a new cricket club in Torquay.

Mr. Stockdale had explained that the Torquay club had been formed last year, and that it had just acquired a new ground.

He had come to Plymouth to invite the garrison to be its opponents in a special match to celebrate the opening of the ground on 16th August.

I listened as the captain told me that he had accepted the invitation on behalf of the officers who all fancied a trip to Torquay, and a chance to drink the health of their new hosts!!!

He ended by asking if I would like to umpire the match. I thanked him, but declined.

It had been a busy summer, and I sensed that it might be more of a social occasion that a cricketing one! Torquay was not known for producing many serious cricketers!

*

Two days later, Molly handed me a letter that had arrived whilst I was out.

As soon as I saw the envelope, I knew it was from Mr. John!

I tore it open, sensing that it might be important.

It began "My Dear Friend", and then repeated exactly what Captain Rush had told me two days earlier. However, there was much more!

It seemed that, because Mr. John lived so close to Torquay, the club had sought his advice since its formation.

As the secretary of the nearby Teignbridge Club, he had a lot of contacts, and it was he who suggested that Plymouth Garrison be invited to play in the celebration match.

"I am an honorary member," he wrote, "so I can invite you to join the evening festivities, and we will have the time to renew our friendship. I suggested this very match with you in mind!"

Suddenly the prospect of a match in Torquay seemed much more attractive, and, next morning, I called in to see Captain Rush to tell him about the letter, and my change of heart!

*

Three weeks later, the garrison coach pulled up in George Street, and I squeezed in amongst the officers. We bounced over the cobbles and set off up the coast, towards Torquay.

I had never been to Torquay before, but knew that it called itself "The Queen of Watering Places".

I had heard that since the arrival of the railway, people had been flocking there, and, in recent years, I had seen "Special Excursions to the Seaside" advertised in Plymouth.

The coach took the road towards Newton Abbot, and then headed for the coast. The officers, sitting near the windows, promised to shout when they got a sight of the sea… but no shout came.

Suddenly, before we had reached Torquay, I heard the coachman call to the horses, and we shuddered to a halt.

Somebody shouted "They're here", a gate swung open, and the coach lurched across some rough ground before coming to a final stop.

It had been dark inside the coach, and I blinked as I slid along the seat and followed the others out into the sunlight.

We had arrived in a large meadow, which sloped slowly towards a line of trees which formed its lower boundary. The coach had pulled up under the branches of huge oak tree, and right next to a marquee where, already, a crowd was gathering.

I helped the coachman off-load the wooden kit boxes into the visiting team's tent behind the marquee, and then recovered my own small bag, which I had tied on to the roof.

I put on my frock coat, and carefully stowed my four stones, my measuring rod, my chalk, and my knife, into its pockets. Finally, I took my top hat from its box, pulled it down over my eyes, and approved my reflection in the coach window.

I had a reputation to look after and, probably, a big crowd to impress today.

Just as I was admiring myself, I felt a heavy slap on my shoulder and heard a familiar voice.

"What a pretty fellow you are, sir!" said Mr. John, smiling from ear to ear. "Come and meet the groundsman."

It was good to be in Mr. John's company again, and we strolled out to meet a tiny little man who seemed to be pushing a machine that was almost as tall as he was.

"This is George Pearce," said Mr. John, and we shook hands warmly.

George explained that this was a new "Silent Cutter" mower, which the club had bought from a firm in Leeds. He told us proudly that it had a chain which transmitted power from the rear roller to the cutting cylinder as it moved forwards. It certainly looked the part!

As we left him to his mowing, I could see that he was tending an area of newly laid turfs, which seemed to measure about 40 x 20 yards.

The rest of the playing area had been scythed, but was still quite heavily grassed.

The turfs had begun to settle, but recent sun had left them ridged. It was a bad sign, but one that was common to most newly laid cricket grounds.

Mr. John told me that George Nickells, from nearby Barton Farm, had provided a hundred sheep to graze the whole meadow for two days, to make sure it was fit for today's fixture.

This morning, after the animals had left, local boys had earned some pocket-money by pulling out the long stems of coarse grass, which the sheep had rejected.

Mr. John thought that the club had worked hard to turn a meadow into a cricket ground, and I agreed with him.

The groundsman was paid four shillings a week, he said, and he wished they had someone like George Pearce at Teignbridge.

He pointed to some high ground, behind the line of trees on the lower boundary, and told me that this was Windmill Hill. The Torquay club had played there before moving to Chapel Hill Cross, and had brought their groundsman with them.

Whilst we were talking we began to feel some spots of

TORQUAY CRICKET CLUB.
GRAND FÊTE
In celebration of the Opening of the New Ground,
AT CHAPEL HILL CROSS.

THE Committee beg to announce that it is intended to OPEN the NEW CRICKET GROUND, on MONDAY, 16th of AUGUST, 1852, when a Match will be Played between the

THE OFFICERS OF THE GARRISON, AT PLYMOUTH, AND THE TORQUAY CRICKET CLUB.

By the kind permission of Col. FRAZER, the SPLENDED BAND the 35th Regiment will attend, and Perform choice Selections of the most admired Music, commencing at 3 o'clock.

AN ELEGANT AND SPACIOUS MARQUEE,
the Floor well Boarded, will be erected, and towards Evening thrown open
FOR A SOIRÉE DANSANTE.

LADIES' PATRONESSES.	STEWARDS.
LADY YARDE BULLER,	L. PALK, Esq.
MRS. PALK,	R. S. S. CARY, Esq.
MRS. CARY,	H. C. M. PHILLIPPS, Esq.
MRS. HARRIS, *Rooklands*.	CAPT. STORY,
MRS. STORY,	CAPT. PHILLIPPS,
MRS. BELFIELD LOUIS.	F. M. LYTE, Esq.

Ladies' Tickets, 4s., Gentlemen's 5s. including Admission to the Ground.

Admission to the Ground, 1s.—Tickets to be obtained of the Secretary, Committee, and at the Libraries, Torquay.

A Special Train will leave Exeter, at 8.20 A.M., calling at all Stations, and arriving at Torquay, at 10.

Also a Special Train from Plymouth, at 8 A.M., calling at Ivybridge, Kingsbridge Road, Totnes and Newton, arriving at Torquay, at 10.

These Trains will leave Torquay, at 9.20, P.M.

REFRESHMENTS WILL BE PROVIDED ON THE GROUND.

W. H. KITSON, Secretary.

The notice announcing the opening of the new cricket ground at Chapel Hill Cross in 1852.

rain, but now it was growing heavier. We looked at each other, grimaced, and began to run towards the marquee.

I got there first, pushed open the canvas flaps, and ran headlong into a hive of activity.

The marquee had a boarded floor which exaggerated the sound of the footsteps of those who were running in all directions, erecting a stage for tonight's soiree.

A lady wearing a bustle hurried towards us making hand gestures, and ushered us back out into the rain. Already queues of people were paying their shillings and coming in through the top entrance to the ground.

Traders were setting up their tents around the playing area, and Marley's catering outlets were surrounded by customers sheltering from the weather.

Mr. John and I were standing under the giant oak tree, where the garrison's coach was parked, when suddenly he shouted "Williams!"

A tall, thin man in his early twenties stopped in his tracks and made his way towards us.

He was wearing an old black coat, and, as he approached us, I noticed that he had a mop of mousy brown hair, and two large protruding front teeth.

"This is Williams, your fellow umpire," said Mr. John, and turning towards the young man, continued, "This is the garrison's umpire, M.C.C. registered, and my guest today."

Williams looked overcome, but managed to mutter, "Pleased to meet you, sir."

Mr. John explained that Williams had been the only person to answer the club's advertisement for an umpire, and that today's match would be the first time he had been appointed to a senior club fixture anywhere.

His father had umpired at the nearby St. Marychurch club for many years, and had taught his son to follow in his footsteps. Williams was warming now, and smiled at me proudly.

It was past ten o'clock, and I explained to Mr. John that it was time for me to begin the pre-match preparations.

I invited Williams to follow me, and we headed for the garrison team's tent where Major Batten was already waiting for me.

The rain had eased a shade as we walked out together to the turfed area, where George Pearce left his mowing to join us.

The whole area was quite densely ridged, but after a while I found a small patch, near to the top, that seemed to be flatter than all the others. Then, taking two paces back, I asked the major for his consent, took out my knife, and cut the bowling crease.

George could now mark the remaining creases to tally with it.

Finally, I needed to decide whether the match could start at eleven, as scheduled.

As a point of politeness, I thought I should discuss this with the Torquay club secretary, Mr. Kitson, and found him in the marquee, directing operations there.

Mr. William Kitson was a local solicitor, now in his early fifties, and one of the most influential men in this rapidly growing town.

Mr. John had told me that he was the driving force behind the new club, and had even offered to fund the purchase of the new ground himself, if that turned out to be necessary.

"Forgive me, sir!" I said. "I'm mindful of the rain, and inclined to delay the cricket until after lunch is taken." He smiled, took off his top hat, and seemed to recognise me.

"Of course! So be it! John has told me that your judgement should never be faulted!"

I thanked him, turned around, and told Williams to run off and notify the two captains of the delay.

The rain was lighter now, and I guessed that the crowd had grown to almost a thousand.

Tables had been set up in one corner of the marquee, and, already, some of the players had sat down and were beginning to pass the jugs of cider from one to another.

Mr. John was sitting with Mr. Cary, the chairman of the Torquay club, and I could see that they were already eating. He signalled for me to join them, but I smiled, mouthed my thanks, and declined.

My mind was rushing back to Teignbridge, five years ago, and that bench under the eaves of the pavilion, where I sat alone with my thoughts while others feasted.

I made for the door, pushed aside the flaps, and looked for Williams. Sure enough, he was sheltering under a chimney-sweep's cart, which had been left near the oak tree.

"Stay there, Williams," I shouted, "I'll get us an elevener."

He gave me a toothy grin, and I went back inside. I found a young man in a red tunic and asked, "Are you with Marley's caterers?"

"And proud to be so sir," he replied.

Handing him a shilling, I asked him for two cold meat pies and two pots of ale, "and no delay". He hurried off, and soon returned with a dish covered with a white cloth.

I took it from him, and made my way out to my fellow umpire. Williams saw me coming, shifted to his left, and made a space for me to join him.

"When we call 'PLAY', I want you to stand tall, my friend," I began. "Just like your father would want you to!" He was looking at me now, and giving me his whole attention.

I knew he would be nervous about today, but tried to give him the confidence to make his own decisions.

I asked him if he had any real worries about the job he was soon to tackle, and after some thought he replied, "Well, I knows the laws, sir, but I ain't too sure if there been any new ones since I learn'd 'em sir!"

I reassured him that there had been no major changes in the laws for six years now, but told him of a letter which I had received from the M.C.C. late last year.

Ever since round-arm had become legal, eighteen years ago, bowlers had enjoyed the chance to bowl faster. But now, in a never-ending quest to bowl faster still, they were beginning to take advantage, and the M.C.C. was worried!

"It is the wish of the Committee that any M.C.C. member who shall stand umpire in any match shall pay particular attention to the bowling in reference to Rule No. 10 of the Laws of Cricket, and if any bowler shall, in his opinion, transgress the Law by throwing or jerking the ball, or if the hand of a bowler shall be above the shoulder in delivery, he shall call 'No Ball!'"

I warned Williams that, in Devon, many bowlers were trying to gain this advantage, and, if a "No Ball!" was called, were simply changing ends to test the views of the other umpire!

If this happened to us today at Chapel Hill Cross, we needed to support each other!

Williams stared at me for a moment, as though he was analysing my words, and then replied, "If you's to do it sir, you may s'pose I'll do it too, sir!"

We had finished our pies while we were talking, and the rain had stopped now.

As we climbed out from under the cart, we could see that

the ground was filling fast from the top end, and that play was now possible.

I went back into the marquee and found Mr. Kitson deep in conversation with a number of other dignitaries. After a moment, he noticed me standing there, and turned and smiled.

"If it pleases you, sir, play can begin at 12.30," I said.

"So be it," he replied and returned to his conversation.

Mr. John and Mr. Cary were still finishing their lunch, and enjoying a joke together, as I passed by unnoticed.

Williams had not, of course, followed me into the tent, but had remained waiting outside.

I told him that we would be walking out together at 12.20, and asked him to alert the two captains, and to meet me outside the marquee as soon as he was ready.

In a moment or two, he was back by my side, but this time he was wearing a top hat, just like mine!

We were soon joined by Major Batten and the Torquay club's captain, Mr. Julian, and at 12.20 the four of us made our way out to the pitch.

I whispered to Williams, "You're the home umpire, my friend, but I'm here if you need me!"

Williams called the two captains together and Mr. Julian won the toss. He had a look at the pitch, and, unsurprisingly after the recent rain, he asked the garrison to bat first.

As we walked off again, I already sensed that Williams was beginning to enjoy his new role!

At 12.30, the Torquay team took the field, the crowd applauded them every step of the way, and even the sun was shining again now!

Williams and I followed the batsmen out, and I took the top end for the first over.

I checked that the two scorers were seated in their chairs under the oak tree, and threw the new ball to Mr. James Kitson, who delivered the very first ball of a formal match on the meadow at Chapel Hill Cross.

It was a special moment for the newly formed Torquay Cricket Club!

The officers' innings started very slowly. The batsmen didn't trust the new pitch, and felt certain that they could expect a "shooter" at any moment.

In fact, the pitch played better than expected and it was their caution which saw the last man dismissed at nearly 4.30, with the scoreboard showing just 92 runs.

During the ten minutes' break between innings, I changed ends with Williams, and told him how impressed I had been by his performance.

He had called "no ball" on four occasions, and, although it was the bowling end umpire's responsibility, I had agreed with his call each time.

With less than two hours to get the runs, time was against the Torquay team now.

Mr. Collier and Captain Wallack were experienced bowlers, and between them they had limited their hosts to 66 for 3 when Williams called time on a drawn match.

The crowd had been well entertained, and became noisier as the afternoon wore on.

A regimental band had performed from three o'clock, and the cricket had taken second place for a while as everyone sang along to the music. Many lingered on, some sharing a jug of ale, and others simply snoozing in the long grass.

Williams had gone without saying goodbye, but I guessed that this new experience had been exhausting for him.

I was tired too, after a long day, and went over to sit in one of the two scorers' chairs which were both now standing empty.

I watched as the ladies of the Torquay club summoned carriages to take them home to change for tonight's soiree.

The sounds of the carriage horses were drowned by the shouts of the men who were dismantling the booths and stalls, and I began to realise just how much I had enjoyed today.

I must have been smiling because, just then, a voice alongside me said,

"And well might you be pleased with yourself!"

Mr. John had taken the other chair, and was leaning towards me.

"So, tell me, my friend, will your match report applaud us, or damn us?"

Mr. John knew that, as a registered M.C.C. umpire, I had to post a report to Lord's after every match in which I officiated.

"Applaud you without question, Mr. John," I replied. "Kynaston can be a fussy devil, but my report will leave him no room for doubt!"

Mr. John smiled, leant forward again, and then whispered, "But how does your heart judge us?"

I told him that I thought that the meadow would make a fine cricket ground, one day, but of course it needed a pavilion, not a marquee.

Whilst I approved the club's purchase of a mower, and felt that Pearce was doing a good job, I told him that the club urgently needed to buy a roller to help the turfs to settle more quickly.

"And then, all that remains is a horse, with a stout set of horse boots, and your meadow will be a match for your Teignbridge!"

Time passed quickly, but unnoticed, as we sat there chatting together.

The Teignbridge ground would stage the biggest match of its season in exactly one week's time, and I wished Mr. John luck. He had arranged for the All England Eleven to play 22 of Devonshire for the second successive year, and, despite last year's success, he now seemed worried about the prospect.

Although the great Hampshire fast bowler, Sir Frederick Bathurst, had agreed to play for Devonshire, several other key players were away on grouse shooting expeditions.

To add to his fears, Mr. John was uncertain about attracting a big enough crowd to Newton Abbot to justify the cost of the venture. He seemed relieved to be able to share his concerns with me.

Whilst we had been talking, the ground had almost emptied, and neither of us had noticed the time until Mr. John pulled out his pocket watch.

"I must off and change my coat before Charlotte arrives," he said, and shook my hand.

"Look out for her carriage. She will be prompt, you may depend upon it!" he added, as he strode off towards the marquee.

My coat was quite smart enough for the soiree, but I decided to go back to the coach to put my top hat back into its box. I certainly didn't want to be recognised as today's umpire, if I was to mingle with the nobility of Torquay!

The coachman was asleep in the box seat, but I managed to open the door quietly, and leave him undisturbed. He wouldn't sleep for long, poor fellow, once the band had struck up!

By the time I had returned to the marquee, carriages and traps were arriving, one after the other.

The gate to the meadow had been left open, and the drivers were taking the direct route across the outfield to the marquee entrance. I could only imagine what Pearce might say when he came to work tomorrow!

I pushed my way between the horses, and saw Mr. John offering his hand to help Charlotte step gingerly from her carriage.

Carrying her silk dancing shoes in her other hand, she picked her way slowly through the grass, ducked under the flap, and reached the safety of the raised wooden floor of the tent.

Mr. John beckoned me to follow, and we made our way through the crowd to the long table reserved for the club committee.

Just as we sat down, the band began to play and the caterers, in their white coats, began to bring food and wine to the tables.

Platters of chicken, duck, or tongue were soon joined by silver trays of lobster salad, and hot breads. Moments later, the chatter subsided, and was replaced by the clatter of knives and forks as a hundred guests set about getting value for their five-shilling tickets.

I had been seated next to an old man with a short white beard, and, almost immediately, he turned towards me and extended his hand.

"I'm William Trant," he said, "and to whom do I have the pleasure of being a neighbour tonight?"

Luckily, he hadn't recognised me as today's umpire, so I replied, "It's my privilege to be a friend of Mr. Yarde-Buller sir!"

Clearly impressed, he added, "A privilege indeed, young man! Welcome to our new cricket ground!"

Mr. Trant then told me that he was an Old Etonian, a former M.P. and that he now lived in Torquay in a house called "Woodfield". His house had been built in the 1830s for a local man called Edward Vivian, re-using local grey limestone from Torwood Manor.

Perhaps I yawned, but he quickly changed the subject to cricket.

He explained that he had been a founder member of the Torquay Club, and was devoted to absolutely everything connected to cricket.

He asked me if I had been at Teignbridge when the All England Eleven had made its first visit to Devon in 1851.

I told him that work had prevented me from being there, but that I hoped to be there next week for the Eleven's second visit.

"Sir, you missed a show last year, for certain, but I'll relish the telling of it if you allow me!"

He then recounted a story of how, at the Teignbridge match, he had challenged the All England Eleven's John Wisden to a single wicket match!

Wisden was twenty-five years old, one of the fastest bowlers in England, and Trant was a retired local cricketer of nearly seventy! "Did he indulge you, sir?" I asked.

"Indeed he did! But I warrant he didn't relish the beating I gave him!"

I tried not to look too surprised, and concluded that old age was affecting my companion's memory. However, rather than question him, I decided to look impressed, and nodded my approval.

As the evening went on, we discussed the latest ridiculous change to the LBW law, and the recent formation of the United All-England Eleven.

Whilst we were talking, fruit tarts had been served with iced champagne, and the chatter around us had grown louder and louder.

Just when we had begun to shout to be heard, the crash of a gavel on the end of our table brought the room to a sudden silence, and William Kitson got up to speak.

After welcoming the ladies and thanking the caterers, he congratulated both teams on their contribution to this momentous occasion.

He announced that the club now had sixty-five full members, and hoped that others would join after visiting the club's new ground for the first time. The town was growing fast, and now deserved its own cricket club.

He said that the officers of the Plymouth Garrison had lived up to their reputation for being the perfect guests for an opening day celebration like this one, and that he hoped fixtures between the two clubs would become a regular highlight of the season, in years to come.

He ended by thanking Mr. Palk for providing the marquee, but hoped that the club would build its first pavilion when the necessary finance could be arranged.

As soon as he sat down, the band filled the tent with music, and almost everyone took to the dance floor. I watched Mr. John and Charlotte join in for a lively Waltz, and then lead the floor into what the band leader called a Bohemian Polka.

It was fun to be amongst so many people enjoying themselves, and a completely new experience for me.

All good things come to an end, and, at about 10.00, Major Batten called the room to silence once again, and thanked the club for its hospitality.

He looked forward to visiting again soon, and wished the club every success in converting what he called a "charming meadow" into a "capital cricket ground".

Whilst the room applauded its visitors, I grabbed the chance to kiss Charlotte's hand, and to thank both Mr. John and Mr. Trant for a wonderful evening.

As we made our way towards the exit, the band played the popular minstrel song "De Camptown Races", and almost everyone was stamping on the wooden floor to the chorus "Do Da… Do Da", as we filed out into the night air.

Luckily for me, we were giving no lifts tonight, and I managed to squeeze into the coach before the coachman put his boot against the door to close it.

The horses had been well rested, and we set off quickly from under the oak tree, past another oak at the top of the ground, and then on to the open road.

It wasn't long before the chatting subsided, and sleep took over.

The head of the officer on my right lolled on to my shoulder, and I began to recall the highlights of what had been a remarkable day.

CHAPTER FIVE

At the end of every summer, the dockyard becomes busy with ships, and there is usually plenty of painting work to be done.

August 1852 was no exception, and, soon after returning from Torquay, I found myself working twelve-hour days, either up ladders or on my knees!

Earning money whilst it was on offer took priority now and in the circumstances. I was pleased that the garrison's cricket season had all but ended.

I had told Mr. John that I would try to come to Teignbridge on the following Monday to watch the All England Eleven play against 22 of Devonshire, but soon realised that I had no chance of being there.

Some days later, I bought *The Western Times*, and as expected it had published a match report. My heart sank as I read it, and I felt so sorry for those at Teignbridge who had invested so much time and money into arranging it.

The attendance had been disappointing, and the pitch had behaved badly, just as Mr. John had feared.

The match had begun well with the All England Eleven scoring 158 in its first innings.

Mr. Collier and his brother, who had both played for the garrison at Torquay, had shared in the dismissal of the great George Parr, caught by one and bowled by the other! What a celebration they must have enjoyed!

However, on the second day, the pitch deteriorated so badly that the 22 Gentlemen of Devonshire were bowled out for just 88, with only two batsmen reaching double figures.

The final humiliation came on the third day when both teams managed only 42 runs each when they batted again!

Those turfs had never settled, and the club was paying the penalty for failing to employ an experienced groundsman.

Mr. John had been clean bowled in each innings by William Clarke, for nought and one.

Reading on further, I noticed that Fred Bell had not been asked to umpire this time, and guessed that Clarke had insisted that the hosts provide an M.C.C. registered official.

That night I lay in bed wondering if I might ever see the world's finest cricketers playing in Devonshire again!

If I had told Mr. John that I was available, would he have asked me to take Fred Bell's place? Had I missed the chance of a lifetime? I would never know!

*

Christmas came and went, and this current year began with some heavy snowfalls.

The garrison had asked me to carry out some indoor decorating, and, because work at the dockyard had been slowed up by the weather, I agreed to do it.

Almost as soon as I got there, Captain Rush sent a message asking me to come to his office. He wanted to know all about my visit to Torquay and, as soon as I was seated, he began to fire questions at me.

How was the new ground? How did the pitch play? Had I met William Kitson?

Had I been invited to the soiree? Did Major Batten discuss a regular fixture?

I remembered every moment of the day, and was able to answer him at length.

As I got up to leave, he asked if I had met an old fellow called William Trant.

I smiled, and told him that we had spent the whole evening together!

"He told me a tale of John Wisden, but I laughed and gave it no credence," I said.

"He's a rummy old cove for sure, but you should know he's a truthful one too!" replied my host, and then told me the whole story.

Trant was a keen follower of cricket, but, despite his age, believed that he was still a fine player. Some of the All England Eleven had met him before, and, perhaps because of his white beard, referred to him as "Old Father Time".

Just before the match at Teignbridge was due to begin, William Clarke had to stand down after suffering from an attack of gout, and Trant immediately offered himself as a replacement.

When Clarke politely turned down his offer, Trant was so disappointed that John Wisden, who was standing nearby, offered to play a single wicket match against him, as a consolation.

The match was announced and the crowd welcomed the extra spectacle.

THE MEADOW AT CHAPEL HILL CROSS

William Trant – A painting by Nicholas Felix in 1851

Wisden won the toss in front of the huge crowd, and chose to bat first.

After scoring one, he purposely dragged the ball on to his wicket. The delighted Trant then took up the bat, and, with a magnificent cut shot "won" the contest.

Bell's Life reported the incident with tongue in cheek, remarking that Wisden "was not a match for his renowned opponent, whose play has been the subject of much praise for the last sixty years!"

The match had been so carefully arranged that, ever since, Trant had told the story of how he had conquered the "champion cricketer of England".

Nicholas Felix, who played for the All England Eleven that day, was so amused by the occasion that he painted an image of the old man to commemorate it!

He had captioned the painting "The Castle of O' Trant O" after the novel by Horace Walpole. As always, the humour was obvious, but never unkind.

Still smiling at the story, I said goodbye to Captain Rush and promised to finish the decorating. We would meet later on, to discuss the new cricket season.

*

Whilst life in Devonport remained fairly dull, the same could not be said of life at Torquay Cricket Club, and, in early March, I received a letter from Mr. John.

It seemed that after the disappointing match against the All England Eleven, the Teignbridge committee had decided not to invite them back in 1853.

Mr. John saw the decision as being cowardly, and had

written to the Torquay club suggesting that it might like to take over the fixture!

Teignbridge had been paying £90 per match to secure the services of the Eleven, and Mr. John felt that, in a growing town like Torquay, it would be easy to recover that sort of outlay.

At first, Mr. Cary, Torquay's chairman, was not keen, but when William Clarke offered to drop his price to £80, he agreed to discuss it with his committee.

A special meeting was held on 14th March, and the proposal was accepted.

On the following Saturday, a public meeting was called at Hearder's Hotel, and all Torquay residents were invited to be there to discuss the project.

Mr. Harris presided, and told the gathering that £33 had already been promised.

A huge amount of interest was expressed, and, in his final summing up, he said that the match *would* go ahead, but that the club would not confirm that with Clarke until at least £80 had been raised.

Mr. John's letter ended with a promise that "Further news will follow!"

I shared the letter with Molly, and could scarcely contain my excitement.

This time, I would make sure that I saw these great cricketers in the flesh, just in case I never had another chance of doing so!

On the following day, I used my lunch hour to hurry up to the garrison to tell Captain Rush the news. I knew that he would want to be the first to hear.

I reached his office out of breath, and he offered me a glass of water.

"Some happenings at that new club sir!" I began, and blurted out the whole story.

Captain Rush let me finish, then stood up and came towards me.

Putting his hand on my shoulder, he said, "I'm pleased to know it, my friend," then walking back to his desk, he added, "But some happenings here too, I fear."

He sat down, and before he spoke, I sensed that he had some bad news for me.

It was bad news indeed!

Leaning towards me, he whispered that the garrison commander had heard from the War Office that the tensions arising from Russian pressure on Turkey were becoming a serious threat to British commercial and strategic interests in the Middle East and India.

The whole garrison had been put on alert, and was preparing to take part in large-scale manoeuvres within a month or two.

Because of all this, no cricket matches had been arranged for the coming summer, and only internal matches between the officers would take place.

As I made my way back to the dockyard, my mind was in turmoil.

Cricket had been part of my life for so long now, and I wondered how I would manage without it.

Although Captain Rush had sworn me to secrecy, the newspapers were now confirming exactly what he had told me.

In early April, Lord Stratford, the British ambassador to the Ottoman Empire, sailed to Constantinople to tell the Sultan to reject a proposed treaty with Russia, in what was seen as a further step towards ultimate conflict.

When I got home that night, I told Molly that my painting and my umpiring duties at the garrison would almost certainly cease until the military alert was over.

She smiled and said that we had managed before, so we could do so again!

*

A few days later, just when I was preparing myself for a miserable summer without any cricket, another letter from Mr. John dropped on to the mat.

I held my breath and tore it open! I just prayed for some good news!

In his bold handwriting, he wrote that a second A.G.M. of Torquay Cricket Club had been held on 4th April, and the match against the All England Eleven had been confirmed, and would take place on the 22nd August.

The Committee had asked Mr. John to captain the 22 of Devonshire and to pick the team, and then, surely not… No! It can't be… the letter ended with the words

"I am desirous that *you will act as our umpire.*"

I sat there for a moment in a daze, staring out of the window but seeing nothing.

It slowly dawned on me that, instead of facing an empty summer, I might now be about to realise my wildest dream!

*

The rest of April passed quickly, and, fortunately, work at the dockyard increased as the prospect of a war became ever more real.

I hoped that Captain Rush had heard of my appointment, but had decided that I should stay away from the garrison whilst it was in such a state of turmoil.

Then, one day in the middle of May, I received two letters.

The first was from Mr. John, confirming my £4 fee for umpiring the match, and telling me that the club would also pay my lodgings for two nights.

He went on to tell me that, on 9th May, the club had passed a resolution to build a pavilion on a site at Chapel Hill Cross, yet to be selected by the members.

It would be a two-storey building, with a thatched roof, and a main room which would measure not less than 35 x 20 feet.

The committee had budgeted to spend no more than £130 on its construction, and the money would be raised by the sale of £5 shares, bearing interest at 5%.

The completion date was set for the 1st August… in time for the big match!

The second letter was from Captain Rush saying,

"You are well worthy of the responsibility that I hear has been entrusted to you. Wherever fortune takes me, I will be mindful of you in August."

I will always treasure that letter!

June turned out to be very warm, and, at the dockyard, painting in the sunshine was often unpleasant. Each day we prayed that we were painting hulls, not decks!

As the month wore on news from Constantinople worsened, and then in July we heard that Britain was sending a fleet to the Dardanelles to join up with a similar fleet sent from France!

Devonport was becoming heavily involved, and has remained so ever since.

THE MEADOW AT CHAPEL HILL CROSS

Coaches from London are on our streets every day now, and hansom cabs deliver important-looking people to the garrison at all hours.

But who cares what happens in the rest of the world?

Tomorrow I will be in Torquay, umpiring the All England Eleven, and the Turks and the Russians can do just as they please!!

*

I had now been reminiscing for several hours, and the sun told me that it was almost midday. One boot was hanging off, and the wall was digging into my back! I rested my head in my cupped hands, and stared out over the water.

Just as I did so, I heard a woman's voice in the distance.

"Round and Sound, Five Pence a Pound," she cried, and, slowly her voice became louder. A few moments later, she came round the corner, and I could see that she had a wooden tray hung from her neck.

"Round and Sound, Five Pence a Pound," she cried again, and I beckoned her towards me.

I took the coins from my waistcoat, passed them to her, and held out my hands. She smiled, and filled them with bright red cherries.

"From the Garden of England, sir," she said as she went on her way.

It was warm, and the grass was comfortable to sit on, so why move on yet?

I wondered where the All England Eleven would be just at this moment, and spat out a cherry stone on to the footpath.

Bell's Life had published the Eleven's busy August schedule, and I had memorised it in detail.

It had begun at the Oval against the I Zingari Club.

On the 4th August, it had played a match in Spalding, and then travelled on for further matches in Nottingham, Leeds, and Canterbury, before arriving in Bath for a match against 22 of Lansdowne which will have ended yesterday.

It didn't seem like seven years ago that I had first read that William Clarke, the Nottinghamshire cricketer, was forming a team called "The Eleven of England" to play matches up in the north.

I had chatted about it to Captain Rush at the time, but neither of us had realised just how successful it would turn out to be.

One by one, the finest professional cricketers in England had joined up with Clarke, who offered them a full summer's employment, and more money than either the Marylebone Cricket Club or their own counties.

In recent years, the railway network had expanded, and Clarke had been able to arrange matches throughout the length and breadth of the country... even into Devonshire!

Clubs throughout England were begging for fixtures, and Clarke had slowly raised his asking price accordingly.

It was rumoured that he kept most of the profits for himself, and refused to pick anyone who disagreed with that policy!

He had changed the name of the team to "The All England Eleven", and, wherever the team played, thousands were coming out to watch cricketers whose images and reputations were turning them into national celebrities.

Alfred Mynn, the fastest bowler ever seen, George Parr, the Lion of the North, and Tom Box, the greatest wicket-keeper in England... who would begrudge paying to see his local team measure its skills against giants like these?

But for me personally, one man stood out above them all,

and that was William Clarke himself. He was without doubt the most successful bowler of all time!

I had read so much about him, and tomorrow I would meet him in person.

After leaving school, he had become a bricklayer and had joined his local club in Nottingham.

In his twenties, he improved his skills as an under-arm bowler, and soon turned professional, earning his money in local cricket and sometimes for his county.

Before he was thirty, fortune struck him a cruel blow! He lost his right eye in an accident whilst playing fives, and his batting suffered accordingly.

However, never a man to be beaten easily, he kept on playing local cricket, and, in 1937, married the widow who kept the Trent Bridge Inn.

After the marriage, he developed its back garden into a venue that now staged all the important matches in Nottinghamshire.

Anxious to earn his own living, and now forty-seven years old, he moved to London, and became a ground bowler at Lord's, spending his days bowling to wealthy members who came in for net practice.

The following year in 1846, now often known as "Old Clarke", he had the idea of forming the Eleven of England, and, being based at Lord's, he was able to persuade the very best cricketers to join him.

Ever since he had lost his eye, he had devoted hours and hours of his time perfecting the art of slow bowling, and, tomorrow, at the age of fifty-four, he would show the 22 of Devonshire a degree of skill that had never been seen in cricket before… and I would be there, dearly hoping that he might bowl a few overs from my end!!!

As the afternoon wore on, a cool breeze began to blow over the water and it gave me the energy to get up and stretch before making my way back home.

As I left "the lines", my mind was still posing cricket questions.

"Who will be my fellow umpire?" "Will Alfred Mynn bowl from my end?"

The bustle of George Street and the sound of wooden wheels over cobbles soon brought me back to my senses, and it was quite a relief to get back to St. Aubyn Street and my front door.

I had saved some cherries for Molly, and her cleaning work was now finished for another day.

I would be gone tomorrow, and wouldn't be back until late on Wednesday night, so we had lots to chat about before Molly prepared the tea.

Molly's sister would be staying here whilst I was away, so, after packing my bag, I needed to clear out a cupboard for her, and then get an early night.

Once tea was over, I went upstairs, and knowing that I couldn't afford to forget anything, I began packing slowly.

First, I packed my standard equipment of four stones, a measuring rod, a ball of chalk, and, finally, my knife.

Then I sat on the bed trying to remember what else I might need for the biggest game of my life, and found it hard to concentrate.

In the end, I settled for a folded copy of the 1845 laws of cricket, and a small box of snuff! My overnight items went in on top, and my bag was ready to go.

Luckily, my everyday clothes were smart enough to use while umpiring, and my black coat was still almost like new.

I selected a pair of brown trousers to go with it, and, because I wanted to impress, I decided to add a cream-coloured waistcoat, and a black silk neck scarf!

I would carry my top hat separately, in its usual travelling box.

Molly approved of my choices, and, knowing that I would be leaving early tomorrow, had prepared some sandwiches for me to take with me.

I wished her goodnight, and fell asleep wondering just what tomorrow had in store for me.

CHAPTER SIX

I crept out of the house at six o'clock, without disturbing Molly, and headed for Plymouth station.

It wasn't far to Millbay, but anyway I was lost in thought, and hardly noticed the journey.

The station was full of people waiting for today's first excursion train to take them to Torquay, and I was pleased that I had already bought my ticket.

The train itself had halted at the ticket platform, a hundred yards up the line, and inspectors in uniform were climbing up into each carriage to check the passengers' tickets before they got to the main station and left the train.

Ten minutes later, a whistle blew, and the train slowly pulled into our platform.

The crowd surged forward, and the area became a sea of bodies as those arriving tried to leave their carriages and others tried to grab their empty seats.

I made my way through the mayhem, and on towards the back of the train, where the cheap third-class compartment was already half full.

The "people's" carriage was open on all sides, but had a low roof, on top of which you could store your luggage whilst in transit.

Luckily there were a few spaces left on its central bench, so I sat down, and tucked my bag and box behind my legs.

It was only my second railway journey, and already it promised to be just as uncomfortable as my first!

Very soon, the carriage filled up and the late arrivals were forced to stand, clinging on to the roof rail above them.

After a few more minutes, the guard leapt up into our carriage, climbed up on to the roof, and took his place amongst the boxes and bags above us.

He crawled to the end of the coach, stood up, and waved his flag at the driver.

Just as he sat down, the engine released a huge cloud of steam, and the whole train shuddered and lurched forward.

The passengers who were standing up in front of me fell backwards, and most ended up in the laps of those seated behind them. My head slammed against the head of the man sitting next to me, who seemed to be a priest, and I blurted out an apology.

He looked up at me and muttered mournfully, "We, who cling to the lower spokes of Fortune's ladder, must put up with such things and be thankful!"

But our discomfort didn't last for long, and most of my new companions, who were off for a day at the seaside, seemed determined to make the best of every moment of it.

By the time we reached Ivybridge, the compartment was alive with singing, whistling, and plenty of swearing.

The priest, sitting next to me, tried not to notice, and had begun to fiddle nervously with his rosary.

The bang, bang of the carriages bumping into each other seemed to get louder as the train gathered speed coming down the hill into Kingsbridge Road station.

More people crammed into our carriage, which was now so full that this time the jolt as we left the station made no impact whatsoever!

The train stopped again at Totnes, and then at Newton Abbot, before it finally pulled slowly into Torquay station.

The guard climbed off the roof above us, and jumped down on to the platform.

He ran to the front of the train and unlocked one door of the first-class carriage. As its passengers disembarked, one by one, he checked their tickets before they were allowed to escape the thick clouds of steam which were now enveloping the station's single platform.

It was a long, tedious process, and one which most of the third-class passengers were not prepared to endure. One or two showed the way, and, before long, almost everyone had climbed out of the carriage, and followed them over a low wooden gate and on to the road beyond it.

The priest and I sat waiting for the guard to reach us, eventually showed our tickets and stepped out of the train into Torquay, at last.

Mr. John had told me how to reach the ground from the station, so I set off with my bag over my shoulder and my hat box hung from my belt behind me.

At first, the main road followed a course between the railway track on its left, and a high wooded gorge on its right.

Perched on the top of the gorge was a tiny chapel, and I could see several people gathered around it, watching our train leave the station.

THE MEADOW AT CHAPEL HILL CROSS

After following the main road a little further, Mr. John had told me to look out for a path on my right signposted "To Chapel Hill".

I found it easily, and followed it as it climbed up steeply, through some dense woodland, and alongside a farmer's field.

Although not far, it had been quite a hard climb, but as the path took me over the top of the hill I was confronted by a sight which made it all worthwhile!

I was looking down on the same meadow which I had left just a year ago, but now there was one big difference… it had become a beautiful cricket ground!

The Meadow at Chapel Hill Cross in 1855

The early morning sun was behind me, and it shone down on a handsome little thatched pavilion, built just where the marquee had been pitched last year.

The ground sloped away gradually towards a ring of oak trees which were overlooked by the distant Windmill Hill.

Just now, the whole area was a hive of activity as tents were being erected, and benches were being placed under the huge oak tree where Williams and I had chatted together.

Even though there was still over an hour before the entrance gates would open, several hundred spectators had gathered, and were laughing and joking together.

I stood for a few moments and could hardly believe I was here.

Today would be the climax of my cricketing life, and I would be umpiring a match involving eleven of the finest cricketers who had ever lived.

Men whose deeds featured every day in *Bell's Life*, and whose names were known in every household in England!

Will I find the courage to apply the Laws of Cricket, however unpopular my decisions might turn out to be?

I drew myself up to my full height, clenched both fists, and as I made my way down the hill towards the ground, I whispered to myself "Of course I will!!"

CHAPTER SEVEN

As I drew closer, I could see that the sheep had done their duty, and that Pearce was already hard at work.

The ground now had two entrance points.

The top gate gave access to the higher end of the ground, offering the shade of several oak trees and relative safety from over diligent fielders, whereas access through the lower gate was cheaper but less discriminating.

A temporary sign had been erected outside the top gate, and it announced that entrance via this gate would cost one shilling, whereas the lower gate entrance was offered at half that price, just sixpence.

Private carriages would be admitted for ten shillings, whilst entry for saddled horses would cost only two shillings… both through the lower gate.

Underneath these announcements, in bold red print, were written the words: "Entry to the pavilion is restricted to club members, and players only!"

The queue at the top gate was now several hundred strong, with still half an hour to wait, but I managed to push my way to the front, and to show my M.C.C. registration.

The policeman, acting as a gateman today, seemed very friendly.

He let me in, and I strolled down towards the pavilion, hoping that Mr. John would have arrived early.

Wooden steps led up to the pavilion, and on to a balcony from where I could see a tall dark-haired man waving furiously. "Welcome! My dear friend" he shouted.

I climbed the steps, and we shook hands warmly.

"Come and share the view," said Mr. John, as he pulled up a chair next to his own.

We hadn't seen each other for a year, so we had lots to talk about.

I told him that cricket had come to a virtual standstill at the garrison because of the threat from the Dardanelles, and he listened thoughtfully.

He had decided to join the South Devon Militia, and would do so in the next few weeks, as soon as the cricket season had ended.

As we looked out towards Chapel Hill, the sun was shining, and the crowd was still growing.

Already, at least thirty local traders were setting up their stalls, and it wasn't long before we had to raise our voices above the noise of men shouting and hammering metal.

Mr. John explained that most of the shops in the town had closed for the day, so that their owners could be here to witness the All England Eleven playing in Torquay for the first time.

Special train excursions had been laid on from Exeter and Plymouth, and club sponsor Mr. Palk had hired out more than forty tents to families and interest groups.

I asked him if he had heard whether the All England Eleven would be at full strength today, and he told me that he expected a strong side, but had heard that Alfred Mynn had picked up an injury while playing for the Gentlemen of Kent at Canterbury, last week. Despite being forty-seven years old now, the crowd would be disappointed by Mynn's absence.

Mr. John went on to say that he had hired three "given men" to strengthen the Devonshire team, and that, at his insistence, they had all arrived yesterday.

He hoped that Billy Buttress and the brothers Robert and Vincent Tinley would strengthen his team sufficiently to ensure that the match lasted three days!

It didn't surprise me that he had hired three professional bowlers… it was becoming quite normal for "gentlemen's teams" to hire bowlers, rather than batsmen, when facing the All England Eleven.

Later today, most of the "eligible" young ladies of Torquay would be seated under the oak tree, next to the pavilion, and no gentleman wanted his admirers to see his bowling hit to all parts of the ground by a well-muscled farmer like George Parr!

In any case, most of the gentlemen who made up the 22 of Devonshire took their weekly practice by batting against their club's professional, and hadn't bowled since schooldays.

Suddenly, Mr. John changed the subject and asked, "Will you do us the honour of being our guest tonight, at the Court? Charlotte is nursing Louisa, so won't be present for the dancing, and my carriage is coming at nine o'clock."

Although surprised, I told him that I hoped Louisa would soon feel better, and accepted his invitation immediately.

I had intended to walk towards Torquay to find a lodging house, but this was a much better option.

Just as I was considering my good fortune, a roar from the crowd caught our attention. We looked up, and could see that the gates had now been opened, and hundreds of people were pouring into the ground from both ends.

George Pearce was fighting a losing battle trying to protect the playing area, and now seemed to have given up completely, as the crowds headed for the stalls and the beer tents.

However, if the stall holders thought they might do some early business, they were wrong because before the first glasses could be filled, there was another roar from the crowd, but, this time, an even louder one!

"They're here... and not before time," shouted Mr. John.

"Forgive me, my friend, but I must go to greet them!"

He ran down the steps, and towards the lower gate, where I could see a "diligence" coach and its four horses making its way through the crowd, and heading towards the tents and marquees on the lower part of the ground.

The All England Eleven had arrived, and everyone wanted first sight of them!

At least a hundred people surrounded the coach as each of the players stepped out on to the grass, waved, and disappeared into the largest of the tents.

Whilst the players were acknowledging the crowd, my attention was drawn to two tall men, both wearing top hats, now striding towards Pearce who was busy mowing the playing area.

My heart missed a beat as I realised that one was William Clarke, but who was the other?

It didn't take me long to realise that the other must be my fellow umpire, and that the two men were now telling the groundsman just where to pitch the wickets.

THE MEADOW AT CHAPEL HILL CROSS

The All England Eleven in its Diligence coach in 1851. A Painting by Nicholas Felix.

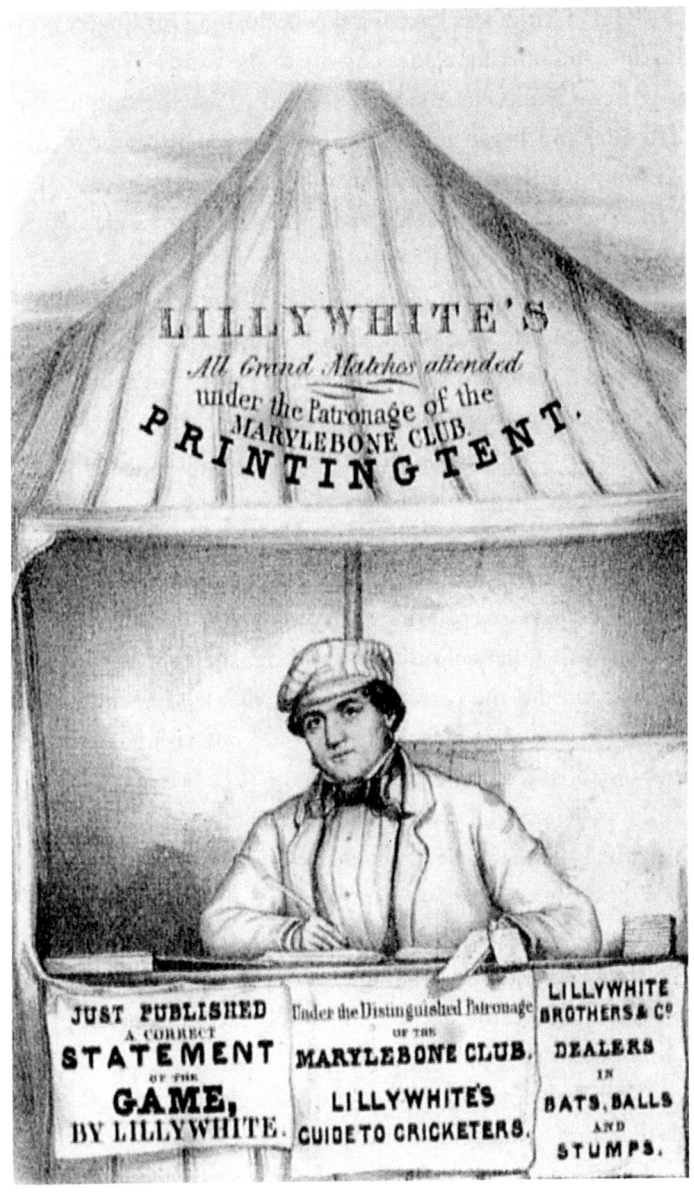

Fred Lillywhite – J.C. Anderson – Lithograph of 1853

"Old" Clarke was kneeling down, pushing his fingers into the turf, and offering blades of grass to the wind.

After a while, he stood up, seemed to ask the umpire for his knife, and began to cut into an area much nearer to the pavilion than the one we had used last year.

George Pearce nodded, and the two men headed back towards the main tents.

As I had stood watching, the pavilion was filling with members, and the crowd had almost doubled.

It was time for me to go, so I picked up my bag and my hat box, pushed my way down the pavilion steps and past the two scorers' chairs and tables, which had already been given pride of place under the shade of the nearest oak tree.

Just below the pavilion, Fred Lillywhite had set up his printing tent, and I could hear a clattering sound as his "portable" press was printing scorecards for the match.

Fred was a meticulous scorer and statistician, who boasted of being "under the patronage of the Marylebone club". His scorecards cost twopence, and you could buy an updated card after lunch, and at the end of play.

He attended all the "grand" matches, and also offered individual scorecards which could be posted to friends (a name & address plus six postage stamps) or a card from every match of the season (five shillings).

Today, he was busy leaning out over the counter of his tent to hand out the cards, and cursing loudly each time he dropped a coin or two on to the grass below.

Next to the printing tent, there was a ginger beer stall, then a stall selling "New season local apples".

Further along were the liquor booths with their ale barrels stacked high outside them, and refreshment tents serving meat sandwiches, and selling cups of tea from big pots.

The sound of chattering and laughter was growing louder and louder.

I pushed past red-faced farmers shouting to distant friends, stern-looking women dragging screaming children, and old men hobbling along, muttering under their breath.

It seemed that everyone in Torquay had taken the day off to be here today, and it was quite a relief when, finally, I left the stalls and made my way to the big tents down by the oak trees which formed the western boundaries of the ground.

Spectators had a good view of the play from here, and Mr. John had told me to look out for the Russian tent, which had been erected yesterday in preparation for the visit of the Grand Duchess Olga and her consort Charles, the Crown Prince of Wurttemberg.

They had arrived in England earlier this month, and had visited Queen Victoria before going on to watch the Review of the English Fleet, at Spithead.

Now the Grand Duchess had come to spend a few days with her sister, the Grand Duchess Maria, at Villa Syracusa, which the Romanoff family had built as a holiday home in Torquay.

The tent was flying the Russian tricolour flag of white, blue and red, and I stopped to watch as uniformed servants were setting out chairs and tables to receive their royal visitors.

A little further along, I reached the marquee which housed the All England Eleven, and then next to it found a small tent marked "Umpires".

One flap had been left open, so I ducked my head and walked in.

Inside were two tables and two chairs, and, there, sat looking straight at me, was my fellow umpire. I recognised him straightaway as Joseph Guy, described once by William Clarke as "the prettiest batsman in all England".

He stood up as I walked in, and offered me his hand.

"Welcome sir, I can see that we are of the same calling! Umpires for our sins!"

His smile was warm, and I liked him at once!

It wasn't long before we were chatting together like old friends.

He had agreed to join the All England Eleven for its August fixtures which had begun in Spalding, Lincolnshire, and would end later this week in London.

He had played in the matches in Nottingham and Leeds, but whilst in Yorkshire, had received a message that his wife had been taken ill.

He had asked Clarke for a few days off to go home to be with her, but promised to re-join the tour as soon as he could.

As it turned out, he had only missed the matches in Canterbury and in Bath, and had managed to catch a train last Saturday in time to play here in Torquay.

Clarke had been annoyed by the inconvenience, and had got his revenge by telling him to umpire today, and by reducing his match fee accordingly!

Joe Guy was a well-built man, tall and upright, and well respected by the cricket world in general. He was almost forty now, and had played for the Eleven since its very first match seven years ago.

As we talked, I sensed that he had something on his mind and wanted to share it.

"Pardon me for askin' sir," he said, "but I have no doubts that you are a man of honour."

Bending forward and, almost in a whisper, he added, "'Tis about Clarke, sir."

He then explained that, after they had selected the pitch, Clarke had told him that he would be bowling from the lower end today, and against the slope.

Joe knew that this meant that he would be expected to stand at the lower end too!

Old Clarke always liked to have his own umpire at his bowling end, in case things started to go wrong!

Joe knew that he would have to allow Clarke's no balls, or face another bout of umpiring at Islington later this week, and he fancied neither of those options! He hated being a stooge, and wanted me to insist on taking the lower end!

"Of course, I will," I said. "Think no more of it!"

This seemed to put him at his ease, and I asked him what he thought of the pitch which both he and Clarke had chosen.

He smiled knowingly and replied, "Not a deuce better than expected, sir!"

Wherever the All England Eleven played, they became used to under-prepared pitches.

Every club in England knew that its only chance of dismissing Caffyn, Parr or Felix when in full flow was to pray for a shooter, or a bad bounce!

Although he would never admit it, I felt sure that Pearce had been given similar instructions!

Just as we were laughing about the inevitability of it all, we looked up.

A dog was barking outside the tent and its bark was growing louder and more savage at every moment. Suddenly, the tent began to shake, and it seemed that its fangs must soon tear it apart.

I was beginning to panic until I glanced up at Joe who was

smiling, and walking towards the flaps. In one movement, he bent down and leapt out into the sunlight, clapping his hands as loudly as he could.

He came back inside laughing. "'Tis Billy with a pot of ale!" he said.

I was no wiser until Joe explained that Billy Buttress was the culprit.

It seemed that Billy, who often played for the Eleven, was a talented ventriloquist, and, after a few ales often imitated dogs or cats.

Traditionally, the professionals call the umpires' tent "The Dogs' Home", so Billy was having a laugh at our expense.

After all that excitement, I looked at my pocket watch and told Joe that it was almost time for me to call the captains for the toss.

I knew that Clarke had his own small tent close to ours, and, as I approached it, I could see that he was already standing outside, waiting for me.

He was a tall man in his mid-fifties, and becoming stouter with age.

He was still wearing his top hat and bow-tie, but had now changed into a grey shirt and trousers.

"I've been a'waiting for you sir," he said, with a hint of annoyance in his voice.

I ignored him, and he followed me through the crowd, and on to the playing area.

Pearce had stopped mowing now, and grabbed the opportunity to have a word with Clarke whilst the whole of Torquay was watching him.

I walked a few paces towards the pavilion and then saw Mr. John waving, and coming towards us.

The crowd was huge now, and had become noisier as it recognised Clarke.

I shook the hands of both captains, and before I had produced a coin, Clarke shook Mr. John's hand, ignored the coin, and said, "Gentleman's privilege to bat first, sir!"

Mr. John thanked him, winked at me, and headed back towards the pavilion.

As Clarke and I returned to our tents, I was surprised to notice that, whilst the crowd cheered Clarke, no one jostled him.

There was no back slapping nor attempted handshakes. He rarely smiled, and I guess that, like me, they weren't sure just what to make of him!

When I got back to our tent, I saw that the original "Umpires" sign had gone, and that Billy had scrawled "The Dogs' Home" all over it!

As I went inside, I noticed that the chairs and tables had gone, and that my bag and hat box had gone too!

Just as I did so, I felt a slap on my back, and saw that Joe had crept up behind me. I jumped, he laughed, and he beckoned me to follow him.

Whilst I had been gone, Joe had moved our chairs and tables into the All England Eleven's marquee. There was plenty of room there, and our bags would be safer.

As I followed him inside, it took me a few moments to take in the scene that confronted me. Everywhere I looked there was a famous face, some smiling, some shouting, some cursing, and others just wondering whoever that was, stood over there!

I found my table, with my personal possessions safely tucked under it, pulled out my bag and began checking all my umpiring bits into my coat pocket.

THE MEADOW AT CHAPEL HILL CROSS

William Clarke – J.C. Anderson – Lithograph of 1852

Joseph Guy – J.C. Anderson – Lithograph of 1852

Just as I was doing so, a big, heavy bag was dropped on to the table next to me.

I looked up, and knew immediately that my new neighbour was Tom Box, the finest wicket-keeper of his generation.

Tom was in his mid-forties, and putting on a bit of weight around the tummy. Even now he was a favourite with the ladies, and grew his hair long, like a twenty-year old.

His team-mates always said that he wore a top hat whilst wicket-keeping because it allowed him to tuck away his curls without flattening them!

"Good mornin' sir," he said, as our eyes met. "I won't be keepin' you."

I didn't mind at all, and relished the chance to watch a top professional prepare himself for the match. I sat on my seat and pretended to be looking elsewhere.

First, he put on a white flannel shirt, with a very long shirt tail at the back.

Then, reaching down, he pulled the shirt tail up between his legs, and secured it to the lowest front button. This created a useful hammock into which Tom packed some soft cloths and spotted handkerchiefs to protect his private parts.

It also meant that he didn't have to pack a pair of underpants!

That done, he put each leg into a belt of India rubber, shaped like a number eight, with a reinforced central bar, and pulled it up and secured it tightly to keep the cloths in place.

He wasn't enjoying all this, and had begun to huff and puff.

I must have been staring, because he smiled and said, "'Tis only this new fast bowlin' that doos it."

Next, he pulled on a very thick pair of white trousers with a leather belt, and then reached into his bag for a stout-looking pair of spiked black boots.

It must have been hard for Tom, who began his career keeping wicket to under-arm bowling. Suddenly, in his late twenties, he had to adapt to the new round-arm style, and face up to bowlers slinging the ball at a much greater pace, and often head high!

It was over ten years ago now since Tom's precious good looks had been rearranged by a short ball at Lord's, which kicked up and flattened his nose! Despite this, he had carried on without gloves or external pads until three years ago. Goodness knows he had resisted for long enough!

All this protective stuff was hard to get used to, but he had a living to make!!

Sensing that time was getting short now, Old Clarke had arrived, and taken up a position just inside the marquee.

I left Tom and looked for Joe, who was in the far corner, fastening his boots.

I waved to him, and he got up and came over to join me.

My pocket watch was showing that it was 10.55 now, so I turned to Clarke and asked him if his team was ready to take the field. He nodded, and we all filed out into the strong sunshine.

The crowd had seen us coming, and a huge roar greeted us as we pushed our way past the carts and then through the families seated on the grass.

Just before I reached the playing area, distant church bells began tolling eleven times. I had dreamed about this moment ever since I umpired my first match on Devonport Hill.

I stopped, shut my eyes, said a little prayer, and stepped out on to the grass to begin a day that I would never forget.

CHAPTER EIGHT

I felt the sun on my back as I walked towards the middle.

Pearce had marked out the pitch, and left the stumps lying by the batting creases. I measured the stumps at the bottom end to be twenty-seven inches, and pushed them into the ground whilst Joe did exactly the same at the top end.

Whilst Old Clarke was setting his field, I beckoned to the scorers to check that they were both seated at their tables, and ready to start. They both waved their consent.

The crowd was so big now that those on the Chapel Hill side of the ground had begun to push forward, to allow others to move in behind them.

For their own safety, I walked over and asked them to retreat by at least twenty feet. They smiled back at me, but no one moved until three stewards ran over to offer their help.

There was some shouting, but foot by foot they drove the crowd back.

In *Bell's Life* recently there has been much talk about marking "perimeter lines" for spectators at grand matches to avoid the accidents caused by fielders chasing the ball into the crowd. Currently, it is getting scant support.

Once the stewards had controlled the crowd, I walked back to the middle where Clarke had set his usual "feathers" field, which included a long-on, a long-off, and a mid-way straight man.

I had read that he employed this field when he intended to throw up a few "tempters" to the early batsmen, and liked to call it his "Prince of Wales feathers".

Up to now, Clarke seemed to have accepted that I would umpire from his end.

Joe had whispered that, as an ex-employee of the M.C.C. himself, Clarke probably respected my registration... but it was still very early days!!

Just as I was wondering when the opening batsmen would appear, a huge cheer indicated that they were on their way.

I had noticed that a big group of young ladies, all dressed in billowing white dresses, had gathered in the shade of the oak tree, next to the pavilion.

As Mr. Beckley and Mr. Kitson came down the pavilion steps together, several leapt up and ran towards the two young men waving and giggling.

Both men stopped, smiled, took off their boaters, and bowed low to their admirers. The crowd screamed its approval!

Today, fun would be their priority, and exciting cricket their consolation prize!

Mr. Beckley was a young man in his early twenties, and had played against the AEE last year at Teignbridge.

But in that match, he had been number twenty-two in the batting order, and now as he stood ready to face Clarke he couldn't hide his nervousness.

Clarke spotted this, and delayed his run up.

When he felt the young man was becoming impatient, he trotted up to the crease with his right hand behind his back, tossed up a high ball that screwed from leg, and followed through until he was no more than five yards from the batsman.

Mr. Beckley pushed forward, and then watched amazed as the ball turned by at least a foot!

The second ball was identical, and, once again, the ball went through to Tom Box.

Clarke was smiling now, as he trotted in for the third time, and this time the ball came through at a lower height, and failed to turn at all.

Mr. Beckley hadn't expected it, and could have hit it wherever he chose to.

The crowd was becoming amused by his confusion, and some began to laugh.

When Clarke reached the crease to deliver the last ball of his over, he stopped for a brief second, and, as he had expected, Mr. Beckley took a pace towards him.

It was too late to stop now, and, as the batsman began to move out of his ground, Clarke tossed the ball high in the air. The ball passed a foot over Mr. Beckley's head, and came to rest just inches in front of his stumps.

I called "over" and Clarke rolled the ball to the other end, and shouted,

"Give these young gentlemen an 'heducation', Topper!"

"Topper" was William Hillyer, a former gamekeeper from Kent, who for the last ten years had been recognised as the best medium-paced bowler in England.

He was forty now, and had earned his nickname for always bowling in a top hat.

Facing him would be Mr. Kitson, a relative of William, the secretary of the new Torquay Cricket Club, and a man in his early thirties.

Although he had never played against bowlers of Hillyer's class, Mr. Kitson had played regular local cricket for Teignbridge and Boconnoc in Cornwall for the past ten years, so stood tall as he waited for his first ball.

For a long time now, Hillyer had suffered from rheumatism in his feet and every year his run-up was becoming more inhibited.

Today, he just shuffled up to the wicket before throwing back his right arm and completing his easy, relaxed, round-arm delivery.

Mr. Kitson played the first two balls defensively, and allowed the last two to pass harmlessly outside his off stump.

At the end of the over, the two bowlers, both wearing top hats, met and chatted quietly as the field changed around.

I have noticed that top hats are still favoured by the older generation, whether bowlers or umpires, because I suppose they imply status. But they are rarely worn by batsmen these days, who worry that they might fall off and hit their wicket!

I watched Clarke carefully, as he moved in to begin the next over.

He was delivering the ball from alongside his right knee, and gave the first ball such a flick off his fourth finger that even the crowd must have heard it.

It pitched outside Mr. Beckley's leg stump, and had Tom Box scrambling on his knees to collect it wide on the off side.

It must have been clear to Clarke that the ball was turning too far on this poor pitch, so he changed his form of attack.

The next ball was a speciality of Clarke's, which is called "The Toss".

It was much faster, and, without bouncing, it was aimed at Mr. Beckley's midriff.

THE MEADOW AT CHAPEL HILL CROSS

Tom Box – J.C. Anderson – Lithograph of 1852

William Hillyer – J.C. Anderson – Lithograph of 1852

The batsman got his bat behind it, but had no chance of scoring from it.

The next ball was identical, and, yet again, Mr. Beckley could only defend it.

Almost three overs had passed now, without a run being scored.

The batsman was becoming desperate, and Clarke knew it!

He trotted in and stopped at the crease for a moment to allow Mr. Beckley to over balance.

He then threw up his "tice" (short for "entice") ten feet high into the air.

The batsman floundered and almost fell, as the ball landed in front of the batting crease. He took a huge swing at the motionless ball, and watched as it rolled slowly out towards Nicholas Felix at cover point. Felix was feeling his age these days, and waited for the ball to reach him before bending down to return it to the bowler.

The batsmen seized their chance, and the Devonshire innings got underway with a single.

If the crowd felt relieved, its relief didn't last for long!

Mr. Beckley's single was to be his last contribution as, in the next over, a delivery from Hillyer hit a ridge, leapt up, clipped his bat, and ended in the hands of George Parr at point.

The ladies under the oak tree tittered behind their fans as he walked slowly back towards the pavilion without giving them a glance.

The next man in was Mr. Mordecai Collier, who was a young man whom I knew well. He lived in Plymouth and had occasionally guested for Plymouth Garrison.

He had faced Clarke in Teignbridge last year, and seemed quite relaxed as he defended his first ball.

With the total on four, Mr. Kitson followed a swinging delivery from Hillyer, and gave George Parr another catch at point.

This brought the charismatic Mr. Compton to the crease, and I could sense that the crowd knew of his reputation.

Unlike most younger men, Mr. Compton preferred to bat without the hindrance of pads and gloves. He had played against the AEE twice before, and on both occasions had posted a good score. He feared no one!

He stood waiting for Hillyer with his bat held high behind him. As the bowler ran in, he rotated the bat in small circles above his head, before bringing it down with a flourish. He hit Hillyer's first ball hard towards Samuel Parr at long-off.

The ball slowed down as it met the long grass, but another run had been added.

Both batsmen were looking fairly comfortable against Hillyer, but neither seemed able to spot which way Clarke's deliveries were going to turn.

Tom Box, who was standing up to both bowlers, and outside the off stump, seemed to be equally baffled. Noticing this, Clarke had brought up his long stop to save the byes.

Mr. Compton was swinging hard at every ball, and, after a few misses, he hit a ball from Clarke right into the crowd. Sam Parr chased after it, but tripped over an old lady as he did so. As he got up, it was clear that he had no idea where it had gone until he heard the crowd chanting "Booth Ball! Booth Ball!"

He rushed into the nearest beer tent, and scrambled about on the floor searching amongst the legs of the patrons who were probably totally uninterested.

Eventually he found it, and rushed out, only to hear the crowd chanting,

"Seven" then "Eight" as the batsmen crossed once again! They were loving it now!

Those eight runs must have nearly doubled Mr. Compton's score, and he smiled his satisfaction.

Sadly, as so often happens, pride comes before a fall and when he tried to repeat the shot against Hillyer, it ended up in the safe hands of George Anderson at long-on.

Mr. Collier fell to Clarke soon afterwards, and made way for Mr. Hounsell, who had top-scored for Devonshire in last year's match.

He came in to join the first of the "given men", the Cambridge professional, Billy Buttress. Billy was hired for his bowling, and was renowned as being the worst batsman on the professional circuit.

It didn't take him long to live up to that reputation!

He played a ball from Clarke into the leg side, and beckoned Mr. Hounsell to risk a quick run. Halfway down the pitch, he changed his mind, and Mr. Hounsell was run out by ten yards! As he walked off, Billy followed his victim towards the pavilion, with his hands on his head, repeating his apologies. Mr. Hounsell completely ignored him!

Clarke allowed himself the faintest of smiles, for the first time since I had met him.

When Robert "Cris" Tinley arrived at the crease, we had two of the "given men" batting together. Tinley was a young "tearaway" fast bowler, but, just like Billy Buttress, he was not much of a batsman.

Clarke had often hired Tinley in recent years, so knew all about his cross-batted slogging. He told his son, Alfred, who was fielding close behind him, to drop back between long-on and long-off, and strolled back to his bowling mark.

This time, he flipped up a "tice" from under his hand.

"Taste this, young Cris," he shouted as he followed the ball down the pitch.

The ball went high up in the air, and looked certain to land on the stumps, until Tinley's wild swing made contact and the ball flew back into the air behind him, over long stop, and into the crowd without bouncing once!

As Hillyer chased it amongst families having an early lunch, Tinley and Buttress ran six, and the crowd loved it!

Those who had bought a scorecard from Lillywhite were keeping the score, but the rest had just come for a day out, and a sight of some famous faces. The memory of Clarke's bowling being hit into Mum's lap would become part of their family's folklore.

Two overs later, Buttress was caught by Alfred Clarke on the boundary, and a young professional called Brown whom I had never seen before had come to the crease and was playing carefully.

Mr. John had selected a Mr. Meally to play today, but he withdrew at the last moment, and Brown, who was hoping for a contract with the Torquay club, agreed to fill in for him.

Tinley had enjoyed his moment of glory, but in Hillyer's next over he edged a high bouncing delivery into Tom Box's gloves.

As the crowd cheered Tinley back to the marquee, out of the pavilion walked the tall, aristocratic figure of Mr. Charles Hoare.

Eight years ago, Mr. Hoare had been one of the founders of Surrey County Cricket Club, and had become its first captain.

Today he was walking out to do battle with his former Surrey team-mate, Nicholas Felix, and the Surrey professionals Hillyer, Caesar, Caffyn and Box.

As he reached the crease, he may have remembered the day back in 1847 when Surrey played the M.C.C. at Lord's, and he had scored a magnificent 58 off the bowling of Clarke and Hillyer!

Mr. Hoare was a fine batsman, but he was well-known for being impatient.

He was quick between the wickets, but a very poor judge of a run.

If I knew that, Old Clarke would certainly know it too, and that spelled danger!

Mr. Hoare saw out Hillyer's over safely, and then, just as he had been looking so secure, Brown was clean bowled by one of Clarke's deliveries which screwed from the leg side.

It was amazing just how many young batsmen seemed to have no idea of how to defend against Clarke's under-arm screw. Brown had just stood and watched as the ball fizzed into his stumps!

Into the arena now walked a dashing young army captain, twirling his bat as he made his way to the middle. Captain Fyfe was a local man from Newton Abbot. He had played for the South Devon club, and was currently on leave from an up-country posting.

He prepared to face Clarke as if he had no care in the world!

He looked around the field, smiled, and beckoned the bowler to "get on with it".

He defended the last two balls of Clarke's over with complete self-assurance.

With Mr. Hoare and the Captain now at the crease, the pace of the Devonshire innings slowed up noticeably.

Both batsmen were very aware of the current etiquette which rules that "gentlemen" batsmen neither leave their crease to attack slow bowling, nor pull a slow bowler's straight balls to leg. A "gentleman" batsman stands tall and either defends with style, or hits a pitched-up delivery hard in front of him.

This, of course, suits Old Clarke perfectly, and never more than when the AEE play teams like Devonshire!

The score moved forward slowly, and the crowd applauded every stylish stroke.

After four maiden overs in succession, Captain Fyfe elegantly drove a ball from Hillyer towards the young ladies under the oak tree.

Charles Arnold chased after it, but it disappeared into a sea of white crinoline and petticoats.

From my position at square leg, I could see that one of the ladies was sitting on it, and her friends were giggling between themselves.

I should have signalled to Joe to tell him the ball was "lost", but the crowd was loving it, so I allowed seven runs to be made before I called play to a halt.

As I walked back to the stumps, at the end of the over, I could hear the clatter of plates coming from the tents at the bottom of the ground.

I checked my watch, and it was almost two o'clock.

Clarke was ready to bowl, but I stopped him, signalled to the scorers, and removed the bails. As the players walked off, I went over to join Joe.

The crowd was now on its feet, and most were heading for the refreshment tents where an "Ordinary" was on sale for 2/6d.

Menus varied, but I had noticed that most offered drumsticks of fowl, with a ham or a warm salad, and mayonnaise of salmon. Just as well that I wasn't hungry!

THE MEADOW AT CHAPEL HILL CROSS

Joe and I satisfied ourselves with a cup of tea, and a piece of ham with a potato.

We took our lunch back to the players' marquee and found ourselves a table.

Tom Box was already there, and messing with his pads. One of them had burst at its seams, and the hay was strewn on the floor beside him.

Old Tom was now gathering it up and pushing it back into the buckskin, and cursing whilst he did it!

Joe winked at me, and went over to him to sympathise.

When he came back to our table, he whispered that the older Tom got, the more hay he stuffed into his pads!

"'Tis no surprise they burst!" he said. "He 'as a farmyard in 'em!"

Once we had finished our snack, we left the marquee and joined the crowd who were gathering around the nearby stalls.

This morning, Joe had spotted a man selling cricket equipment, and needed a new bat, so we set off to find him… if we could!

Everywhere we looked, there were carts of all shapes and sizes.

It seemed as though every tradesman in Torquay had set up his cart, placed six chairs upon it, and then offered "a prime view" to anyone with a few shillings to part with!

These carts made it hard to see the stalls, but we eventually found our man.

Perhaps because we were both wearing our top hats, he greeted us with "Two fine gentlemen! How can I oblige you?"

Most of his display looked designed for children, but Joe soon explained what he was looking for.

Reaching down to the floor of his tent, the man found three bats which he called "Superior", and laid them on the shelf between us. One was an "Eade" and the other two were made by Aquila Clapshaw.

"You may depend on runs from these, sir!" said the man, as Joe looked closely.

After a few minutes, Joe had rejected each of them. Two were one-piece bats, and, although the other had a splice, it was far too heavy.

As we walked away, Joe explained that spliced bats were becoming popular now because, in the big towns, sports shops were offering re-blading.

Whilst one-piece bats had to be replaced if they broke, spliced bats usually broke at the splice, so only needed a re-blade.

Weight, too, was becoming more and more important as round-arm bowling was becoming faster, and more unpredictable.

Joe explained that he had always used a bat which weighed about two and a half pounds, but now fancied trying a lighter two-pound bat to be able to lift it more quickly, to deflect head-high bowling, rather than try to hit it.

I listened, fascinated by the way that bats were changing as the years went by.

On our way back to the marquee, we passed a betting booth where a man was shouting out some odds to a captivated crowd of potential customers.

Every now and then, someone in the crowd would push through with a handful of coins, and shout something to a clerk sitting in the back of the booth with a large ledger and a quill pen.

"Two for one Mr. Hoare" "Four for one Captain Fyfe" "Ten for one Mr. Buller" "Two for one the hunnnndreddd!" he shouted, over and over again.

Although, of course, I knew that the latest Laws of Cricket, issued by the Marylebone Club in 1845, included four laws on betting, I had never seen it at such close quarters before.

Joe explained that the odds were being offered against each of the remaining Devonshire batsmen.

Mr. Hoare was most people's favourite to end the innings as its top scorer, and the booth was offering two for one against the innings totalling 100 or more.

As I stood there, mesmerised by this new experience, I noticed a man with long hair standing near the front. As he turned round, I realised that it was Williams, the Torquay club's young umpire from my last visit to Chapel Hill Cross.

I told Joe that I wouldn't be long, and pushed my way towards him.

"Who's your fancy, sir?" he asked.

"Umpires have no fancies, my friend," I replied.

He gave me a toothy grin and whispered, "That's Marylebone talk, sir!"

Perhaps he was right, and that cricket remained a rural game down here in Devonshire, despite whatever morals the faceless men from London might want to impose upon it.

Time was passing now, so Joe and I walked slowly back to the players' marquee.

Tom Box was strapping on a pad which he had borrowed from his young Surrey team-mate, Julius Caesar.

He told us that he would try to find a needle and cotton tonight to sew up the one which had burst.

The All England Eleven would be staying at Hearder's Hotel near Torquay harbour, so he was likely to be able to find someone to help him there.

As Tom was pulling on his gloves, Joe told him that he had

just been looking for a new lightweight bat with a splice, but hadn't found what he wanted.

He didn't know of a good bat maker in Nottingham, and the local tent here had nothing much to offer.

Tom laughed, and smiled. "A handsome man like you, Joe, should pay a visit to Eleanor! Nuzzle her neck, and she'll likely give'e one for nothing!"

Joe looked puzzled, and Tom explained that Eleanor Page had a bat factory in Kennington Road, next to the new "Oval" cricket ground, and made the best bats in England. She would make Joe a bat of whatever weight he chose, and fit it with the very latest whalebone splice! But how would he get a bat from London?

After this match had ended, the AEE was playing its next fixture against 22 of Islington, and Tom promised to take Joe to meet Eleanor, in person!

As I was listening to the two chatting, I looked up and saw the silent figure of Old Clarke, standing outside the marquee.

His presence signalled that the lunch break was almost over, and my watch confirmed that the hour was nearly up.

Joe shouted to everyone that we were leaving the marquee, and, soon afterwards, we led a motley band of professionals through the cheering crowd and out on to the ground once again.

CHAPTER NINE

As the last of the players stepped on to the ground at 3.00, the Torquay Subscription Band began its afternoon entertainment with a lively polka.

The pot boys were still stepping carefully amongst those seated on the grass, and were pouring out a choice of a local beer, or a dark bitter beer called porter.

Fred Lillywhite was selling his updated scorecards, and the crowd was settling down to watch the 22 of Devonshire progress from their lunchtime total of 62 for 8 wickets.

As we waited for the two batsmen to appear, Old Clarke was examining the pitch in great detail.

At first, he was kneeling, and feeling the turf, then standing up and sifting some loose soil through his fingers.

Throughout the lunch interval, the pitch had been trampled on, and in one area it looked as if a jug of beer had been spilled on it! As he walked back to his bowling mark, he passed me and muttered to himself,

"Ridge and furrow, 'tis nought but ridge and furrow!"

As Mr. Hoare and Captain Fyfe walked down the pavilion steps, the crowd gave them a rousing welcome. The beer had hit the spot, and now was the time for some heroics to complete the afternoon!

Mr. Hoare prepared to face the first ball after lunch.

I checked that the scorers were ready, and called "Play".

Clarke trotted past me and, immediately, I noticed a difference in his action.

Instead of delivering the ball from next to his right knee, he hopped as he reached the crease, and delivered this one from under his right armpit.

Mr. Hoare hesitated in his shot, and clearly hadn't expected it.

In the end he played it defensively, and the ball rolled back to Clarke.

Throughout the rest of the over Clarke employed the same action, and he was achieving much more bounce by doing so.

Mr. Hoare had stolen a sharp single off the third ball, and now found himself facing Hillyer's first over after lunch.

At his age, no one regarded "Topper" as quick, but his first ball kept low and crashed into the batsman's shin.

Mr. Hoare was the sort of gentleman who scorned wearing pads, but no doubt had leather strips sewn inside his trousers for protection.

He winced, hopped, and then smiled at the man who had caused him the pain.

Hillyer had been in top cricket for eighteen years and knew how gentlemen reacted to any sort of personal setback, particularly if delivered by a professional!

He ran his fingers over the next ball, and as Mr. Hoare moved into a big off drive, the ball turned away from him, he over-balanced, and Box took off the bails.

The betting booth would have been happy to see him go, but the crowd was silent as he headed back to the pavilion.

Next to join the fray was Mr. Hole, and he received an exceptionally warm reception.

William Hole was one of the founders of the new Torquay club, and a popular figure around Chapel Hill Cross.

As he approached the wicket, Old Clarke went up to him and shook his hand.

Mr. Hole was an able wicket-keeper, and had played for Devonshire against the AEE in both its previous fixtures.

He looked as if he relished the chance of a third meeting, and drove Hillyer's next ball out into the covers for a single.

At the other end, Captain Fyfe was playing carefully, and, although I wasn't keeping the score, I guessed he must have accrued nearly twenty runs by now.

The Captain faced the last ball of Hillyer's over and once again it kept low.

The ball shot along the ground, hit the Captain's front foot, and rebounded out towards the crowd. This time, George Anderson watched its course carefully, and the batsmen crossed just twice before it was back in Tom Box's gloves.

I turned to the scorers, raised my leg and signalled leg byes.

The crowd was waiting for this signal, and I expected their laughter and clapping.

It had only been five years since the Laws recognised leg byes, and crowds all over the country still found this signal very amusing!

It was obvious now that the pitch had deteriorated since the lunch interval.

Throughout the break, Pearce had left the pitch unattended.

I had thought to raise the subject, but realised that it might have been done intentionally now that the Devonshire innings was almost half completed!

During the next few overs, one ball from Clarke would bounce head high, and the next would scurry along the ground. His new action had made the difference.

The batsmen had realised that they had to get their runs quickly now, or fall victim to an unplayable delivery.

Mr. Hole, facing Clarke, had raised his left leg, and played an old-fashioned "draw" stroke, under his leg, and into the crowd in front of the pavilion.

Clarke was not amused and walked down the wicket towards him.

"'Ave a care, sir, or thee'll 'ave an h'accident." Joe heard him and smiled at me.

But it wasn't long before the inevitable happened.

Clarke, still delivering from under his armpit, had rotated his wrist from right to left and bowled three screwers to Captain Fyfe.

For the last ball of his over, Clarke rotated his wrist from left to right and clean bowled the Captain with a ball that turned the other way.

Mr. Hole was next to go after being completely bamboozled by the old maestro. Clarke had bowled him two "tosses", and then he allowed the next ball to roll up his hand before pushing it out using the inside of his wrist.

The action was identical to previous ones, but this time, the ball just looped up in the air at less than half speed.

Mr. Hole had almost completed his drive before the ball reached him, and he lofted a simple catch to George Anderson at cover point.

Vincent Tinley, the third "given man" and brother of Cris, had replaced Captain Fyfe, and now the Honourable Mark Rolle, a very tall, seventeen-year-old Eton schoolboy, joined him.

At the age of six, Mark Trefusis had inherited the vast estates of his uncle by marriage, First Baron Rolle. He was now the life-tenant of the largest estate in Devonshire, which extended to 55,000 acres!

Last year, as required by the will, he had changed his name to Rolle, by Royal Licence.

The Honourable Mark had played in the Eton v Harrow match at Lord's just a month ago, and today, wearing his light blue Eton cap, he awaited the last ball of Clarke's over.

The contest between a privileged seventeen-year-old and a canny old professional of fifty-four had captured the attention of the crowd, and almost utter silence greeted the Honourable Mark's classic forward defensive stroke.

On his estates, he probably hired over a hundred gamekeepers, but today, after Tinley had pushed a single from his first ball, he faced another former gamekeeper in William Hillyer.

For the game's sake, I hoped that this tall young man would entertain the crowd, but it was not to be.

Hillyer ran his fingers over the top of the next ball, and the extra bias from the pitch beat the Honourable Mark's off drive. As his back foot slid out of the crease, Tom Box claimed his second stumping of the innings.

The young man nodded his appreciation to the bowler, and walked off with his head held high.

As he passed the young ladies under the oak tree, some shouted out "Sir", and a delicate little slipper was thrown towards him. He stopped, picked up the slipper, kissed it and offered it back. Four or five young ladies dashed forward to claim it amid squeals of delight from those around them.

Next to come down the pavilion steps was the burly figure of Mr. Montague Bere.

I remembered him well from my first big match at Teignbridge back in 1847, when he took eight of the garrison's first inning's wickets.

Mr. Bere, from the little village of Grimstone, on Dartmoor, was now nearly thirty, and had achieved a lot since those days.

Mr. John had told me that, although not playing so much cricket now, he had qualified as a Q.C. and become a member of the M.C.C.

Mr. Bere defended the last two balls of Hillyer's over, and left Tinley to face Clarke.

Tinley went through life with a smile on his face, and, as a professional, had no hesitation about coming down the wicket to play Clarke.

After missing the first ball, he gave the second "the rush" and hit it right over the crowd on the Chapel Hill side of the ground.

Luckily, someone was strolling around near the fence and threw the ball back while Tinley added three more runs to his total.

Mr. Bere pushed a single off the last ball, leaving Tinley facing Hillyer from down the slope.

Hillyer's very first ball pitched on leg stump and, instead of bouncing, it crept right along the ground and hit his off stump.

Both men laughed as Tinley headed off, knowing that they would both still get paid, and that's what mattered most!

Mr. Gully from near Tavistock was next to bat, but after hitting Clarke's screwer into the crowd for three, he was bowled next ball by a "tice" which arched up towards the heavens, dropped just over his shoulder, and landed on his bails.

The crowd enjoyed it, and even Old Clarke raised a smile at the bewilderment on his young victim's face.

Mr. Martin lasted for three overs before lobbing Clarke's slower delivery into the safe hands of his son Alfred, who was fielding ten yards behind his dad.

Mr. Bere had been batting very watchfully for almost half an hour, before he had a rush of blood, and was clean bowled by a Clarke delivery which screwed from the off side.

At the end of Clarke's over, he looked to throw the ball to Hillyer once again, but saw that his partner was limping off towards the pavilion.

Poor old "Topper" suffered from gout, and sat down on the pavilion steps while he took off his spiked black boots.

The AEE had not brought a twelfth man with them, so Clarke signalled to Mr. John, who was sitting on the pavilion balcony, and, within moments, a young man called Parker ran down the steps to act as substitute.

Parker was a local lad from a village close to Torquay.

Ever since the new club was formed, he had helped out around the ground, and saw his future there.

As he pushed his way through the crowd, one or two of the locals were shouting encouragement, "Show 'em how, Jim" and even "Where's your top 'at Jimmy?"

Clarke had thrown the ball to William Caffyn, and told young Parker to take Caffyn's place at cover point.

As Caffyn strolled back to begin his run-up, I walked over to Clarke and pointed out that, according to Law 32, a substitute could not field at cover point.

Clarke was annoyed at my interference and said, "Beg pardon, sir, but Gawd 'imself don't 'onour such trifles!" I told him that this game was being played under the authority of the M.C.C. and that the Laws do not allow substitutes to bowl, keep wicket, or field at point, cover point, or at long stop.

As he moved young Parker to mid-off, I heard him mutter "Nought but stuff an' nonsense!"

William Caffyn from Reigate in Surrey was probably the finest all-rounder in England at the moment, and bowled his round-arm at a similar pace to Hillyer.

It was well known that he had a strained relationship with Old Clarke, but both suffered their differences for the sake of earning a living.

Captain Mills from the Teignbridge club was the new batsman, and he looked timid at the crease. Although he had played against the Eleven last August, and was wearing pads, he stood like so many other nervous batsmen with both feet well outside his leg stump. Perhaps, like Tom Box, he needed more hay in those pads!

Caffyn's first ball was a toss, and it knocked over Captain Mills' middle stump.

Mr. Coleridge was next to bat, and I had seen him play often. He was still very young, but had guested for Plymouth Garrison several times last year.

He defended the next two balls of Caffyn's over, and then called for a quick run.

Mr. Harris, who had been batting very sensibly at the other end against Clarke, responded but as they crossed, Mr. Coleridge tripped and was easily run out.

The last time that I had seen Mr. Harris was back in 1847, when I made that memorable trip to Teignbridge.

In that match, he had scored 39 runs, and I had been impressed by his hard-hitting style of batting and his total disregard for either pads or gloves.

Mr. Harris lived in Torquay and, like Mr. John, had joined Teignbridge because there were no cricket clubs "for gentlemen" in his home town.

Mr. John had told me that he lived in a big house in Torquay called "Rooklands" and that he was now an important member of the new club. His wife was a club patroness, and he was delighted to be able to play his cricket closer to home.

Joining Mr. Harris at the crease now was another stalwart member of the new Torquay club, Mr. Julian. Since the new club had been formed two years ago, he had already offered to advance funds to help the club to grow, and had been appointed as its very first captain.

Mr. Julian had been selected to play for Devonshire against the AEE last year, but had not enjoyed the experience.

He had failed to score in each innings, and, in the second one, had fallen over his stumps as he tried to put his bat to a "tice" from Clarke.

Today, as he reached the wicket, Clarke had walked up to him and said in a loud voice, "Twice bowled for a cipher was we, sir? 'Twouldn't do to repeat it, would it, sir?"

Although he was always pleased to take their money, behind the façade Old Clarke had no love for privileged amateurs!

Unsurprisingly, Mr. Julian played his first over from Clarke very carefully, rather than give the old boy any further satisfaction.

However, his luck didn't last long before a delivery from Caffyn crashed against his back leg, and knocked him off his feet.

After helping him up, the very next ball found the same spot as Hillyer had found, and Caffyn bowled him with an unplayable shooter.

Poor Mr, Julian had, once again been "bowled for a cipher!"

He got some sympathetic applause from the club members on the pavilion balcony as he made his way back to join them.

As Mr. Julian was leaving the field, I walked over to the scorers to see how the match was progressing. One of them, an old man in a boater, looked up and said, "Two to fall, sir, and one hundred and four notched." I had heard a faint cheer from the crowd not long before, and now realised that those with Lillywhite's cards had been applauding the team's one-hundredth run.

By the time I got back to the middle, the new batsman was not far behind me and, as I turned round, I was greeted by the smiling face of Mr. John.

It was Mr. Harris who was preparing to face the new over, but before Clarke began it, he walked up behind me and offered his hand to Mr. John.

This was the third match which the pair had arranged together, and Old Clarke knew how to greet a benefactor when he met one.

They shook hands warmly.

The first ball to Mr. Harris was a "toss" which the batsman defended in front of his neck. The next two balls screwed viciously from the leg side, and jumped to almost shoulder height. The pitch was becoming almost unplayable now.

Runs were getting hard to come by, and the crowd cheered loudly as Mr. Harris managed to get his bat on to the last ball, and steer it down to long leg for a single.

As the field changed over, I noticed Clarke having a quiet word with Caffyn, who nodded as he prepared to bowl his sixth over from the top end.

Their plot was soon revealed, as Caffyn's first ball was a round-arm "toss" aimed straight at Mr. Harris's chest. The batsman tried to defend it, but as he raised his bat the ball crashed into the back of his unprotected hand.

Blood began to ooze out from just under his knuckles, and he laid his bat down on the grass beside him.

Dear old Tom Box was the first to comfort him, but Mr. Harris was not one to show pain to a professional. He shook his hand a few times, bent forward, and then rubbed his knuckles in the dust to stop the blood flowing.

He allowed the next two balls to pass his off stump, before, once again, stealing a single off the last one.

For all his bravery, Mr. Harris was now looking pale, and as Clarke prepared to bowl a new over, I noticed that the blood was still flowing freely.

Clarke trotted in and bowled another "toss" towards his damaged hand, but this time mercifully it hit Mr. Harris's middle stump instead.

As he slowly made his way back to the pavilion, I wondered how many more of these older amateurs would have to suffer pain before they began to accept that, against modern round-arm bowling, protection was imperative.

As I stood there day-dreaming, the last batsman came down the pavilion steps.

Mr. John Collier was the older brother of Mordecai, who had batted earlier in the innings, and an old friend of mine. He lived in Plymouth, and had guested for the garrison several times in the last few years.

For all his strength and ability as a fast bowler, Mr. Collier was no batsman!

Bell's Life a few years ago had praised his bowling, but summed up his batting in the memorable words, "He hits the ball hard, high, and seldom!"

Mr. Collier had no illusions about his batting skills, and arrived at the crease with a broad grin on his face.

Several of the fielders, who remembered him from last year's match at Teignbridge, were already laughing between themselves.

Last year, he recorded two noughts, and, of course, Old Clarke remembered him too! Unable to resist another insulting remark, Clarke strolled down the wicket, holding the ball in front of him. Then, pointing a finger at the ball, without a hint of a smile on his face, he said, "She's pleased to see you, sir, you may be certain of that!"

Mr. Collier took huge swings at the next two balls, and missed both of them.

For the last ball, Clarke moved every one of his fielders out towards the long grass in front of the spectators. No one was within thirty yards of the bat.

The crowd went silent, and we all wondered what would happen next. I looked round at Clarke, and he was as stony-faced as always.

Mr. Collier had his bat raised high up behind him as Clarke moved in to bowl.

Changing his action completely, Clarke delivered the ball from down by his boots, and he rolled the ball quickly along the ground towards the surprised batsman.

Mr. Collier took his expected swing at it, but, by that time, it had knocked his middle stump right out of the ground.

Clarke tried to stifle a slight smile, the crowd burst out laughing, and the Devonshire innings had come to an end.

Mr. John had not needed to face a single delivery, and, as he walked off with the defeated batsman, he was probably quite relieved.

I removed the bails, and went over to join Joe.

Together, we followed the players from the field, and on

the way stopped to check that the scorers were happy that the innings had been satisfactorily completed.

Most of the crowd were on their feet now, some were going to use the break to top up their glasses, and others, who had predicted that Devonshire would total one hundred or more, were off to queue at the betting booths to claim their winnings.

Joe and I found somewhere to sit down for the ten minutes allowed between innings, and watched George Pearce pushing down the corners of the turfs by hand, then stamping on them.

So much had been achieved at Chapel Hill Cross in a matter of months.

Surely it wouldn't be long before the club bought a heavy roller to solve this groundsman's problems.

The time passed quickly, and Joe went back to the marquee to check that the batsmen were ready.

I knew it must be after 5.00 because the band had stopped playing, so I checked my watch and made my way towards the pavilion.

Before I got there, a roar from the crowd greeted the Devonshire team as it made its way down the steps.

Mr. John threw me the new ball, and led his team out into the late afternoon sunshine. It was a rare pleasure for a captain to have twenty-two fielders, and Mr. John was making the most of it. Soon, there were fielders everywhere I looked!

The first over was to be bowled from the top end, and I watched as Mr. John threw the ball to "Cris" Tinley.

Tinley was only twenty-two, but was already regarded as one of the fastest bowlers in England. He often played for the All England Eleven, but today he was being paid to try to terrorise them!

The two AEE openers were now at the wicket, and Samuel Parr was preparing to face the first ball.

Samuel was a short, stocky man, with a ready smile who knew all about young Tinley.

The Parrs and the Tinleys were brought up together in Nottingham, and were all close friends. They would have to hide that friendship for the next fifty minutes!

Joe called "Play" and Tinley ran in at top speed and hurled the first ball at Parr.

There was an audible gasp in the crowd. Very few of them had ever watched bowling of this pace before!

Parr played it comfortably in front of his chest, and kicked the ball back to the bowler.

The next three balls were just as quick, and Parr allowed them to pass through to Mr. Hole behind the stumps.

The bowler and batsman shared a warm smile at the end of the over, and the ball was passed to Cris Tinley's older brother, Vincent.

Vincent had modelled himself on Old Clarke, and now bowled slow under-arm.

Facing Vincent today was Charles Arnold from Cambridge, who was enjoying his first tour with the Eleven. Arnold was an all-rounder, and hired by Clarke for his ability to score quickly.

Arnold had never faced the older Tinley before, and watched the first ball right on to his bat.

Having spent most of the day umpiring Old Clarke, I could see that umpiring Vincent would be very dull by comparison!

He walked up to the wicket slowly, then crouched right down until his wrist touched the ground before lobbing the ball up to the batsman.

THE MEADOW AT CHAPEL HILL CROSS

Arnold hit his second ball hard, and some poor fielding allowed him a single to get the innings underway.

With Cris Tinley continuing to bowl head-high round-arm "tosses", the scoring rate became very slow.

After about twenty minutes, Arnold became frustrated, and hit a lob from Vincent Tinley straight into the hands of Mr. Kitson at long-on.

The first England wicket had fallen, and the crowd shouted its appreciation.

Mr. John walked over to congratulate the bowler, but must have known in his heart that far greater challenges remained in store than this one!

The first of those challenges, George Anderson, was walking towards them now.

Anderson was a tall, upright Yorkshireman with a thick moustache, and a reputation for being at his best on poor pitches. He relished a situation like this!

Neither batsman was in a hurry, and after the loss of Arnold, neither was going to give away his wicket easily.

Anderson played the thunderbolts with ease whilst Vincent was not getting enough screw on the ball to worry Parr.

A few more singles were added to the total before distant church bells reminded me to check my watch and to announce that the day's play had come to an end.

CHAPTER TEN

As Joe and I followed the players off the field, I thanked the scorers for their support, and handed them the used match ball.

They told me that the score was 22 for 1 at the close of play, and that Arnold had been dismissed for 9.

The day that I had dreamed of for so long had gone well!

Tonight, I would lay in bed and remember every single moment of it!

As I gazed out over this pretty little cricket ground, I felt a nudge on my shoulder. It was Joe with a broad grin on his face. "You're as deaf as an adder, my friend!" he said, pointing to the pavilion balcony where Mr. John was calling to me.

"I can hear the click of wood on leather, and I'm grateful for that!" I replied, and hurried over towards Mr. John, who beckoned me closer.

As soon as I was within earshot, he leant over the balcony and whispered, "Nine o'clock at the top gate, if there's no strangers about." I nodded and thanked him.

As Joe and I made our way back to the marquee, the ground seemed to be full of revellers. Business was brisk in almost every tent, and, outside, families were sitting on the grass, drinking and laughing together.

Fathers in devil masks were frightening their children, and the young ladies from under the oak tree were now holding hands and dancing around it, singing and clapping.

The last trains to Exeter and Plymouth wouldn't leave Torquay station until 9.20 tonight, so there was plenty of time left to enjoy a few more drinks in the booths.

We passed Lillywhite's printing tent where Fred was selling his "End of Day Cards" and there was a long queue of those who wanted a memento of this unique occasion.

It had been a long day, and as soon as we reached the marquee, we pushed aside the flap and collapsed onto the nearest bench.

The caterers from the Union Hotel in Torquay were already busily laying the tables with a selection of meats, and coming and going with bowls of salad and jugs of water.

Some of the players had remained in the marquee since the Devonshire innings had ended, only too pleased to escape the attention of drunken admirers, and the insults of those who scorned anyone who played cricket for money.

The youngsters, Julius Caesar and Alfred Clarke, were already grabbing slices of meat from the table while Anderson and Sam Parr were still untying their pads.

The Tinleys and Billy Buttress had joined us now that the play had ended, and were washing in a bowl of cold water.

I sat there and thought what a privilege it was to be amongst these cricketers, who until yesterday were just the heroes of stories which I had read in the pink pages of *Bell's Life*.

Over in the far corner, William Hillyer had taken his socks off, and his leg was being massaged by a short, stocky man who

I recognised instantly as Nicholas Felix, the president of the AEE.

I had hardly noticed him during the match, but although Felix had been the finest batsman in England for many years, now at forty-eight his playing career was almost at its end.

Born Nicholas Wanostrocht, he had used the name "Felix" to avoid alienating potential pupils from attending the school which he had inherited from his father, and the name had stuck!

Apart from being a teacher, he was a highly talented painter, musician, inventor and author. Last year, he had even written a leaflet called "How to play Clarke".

Felix had been with Old Clarke since the formation of the AEE, and now carried out the role of its president and public relations officer.

Being the only amateur in the team, he had the opportunity to network for the Eleven from inside the pavilions which it visited.

Although Clarke was often invited into those pavilions too, his surly nature more often deterred business rather than attracted it.

Just now, Felix was trying to ease the gout which had struck Hillyer late in the Devonshire innings.

Having drunk a full jug of cider vinegar to ease the pain, "Topper" was now beginning to laugh and joke with those around him.

Seeing his job was almost done, Felix got up off his knees, picked out a violin from his kit box, and headed for the door. As he did so, he turned and waved at us all and shouted, "Until later, my friends!"

Joe told me that Mr. Felix was off to eat with the guests in the pavilion, and "to give them a tune on his fiddle".

THE MEADOW AT CHAPEL HILL CROSS

George Anderson - Illustrated Sporting News 1864

Julius Caesar – J.C. Anderson – Lithograph of 1858

The food in our marquee had been excellent, and after the table was cleared, we pulled up our benches around it.

Young Caesar had persuaded the waitress to bring in four flagons of ale to keep us company, and had handed her a shilling to fill all our glasses.

Joe and Tom Box had pulled out their churchwarden pipes, and were now sending plumes of white smoke into the darkness above us.

Vince Tinley began the conversation by asking if anyone knew a team-mate of his called Tom Nixon. The Parrs and Alfred Clarke nodded, and Joe said that he too had played a few matches with Nixon last year.

It seemed that earlier this year, Nixon, who was something of an entrepreneur, had invented a bat handle which was "springy".

Instead of having a solid wooden handle, Nixon had used canes, and the effect was to reduce the shock of the ball against the blade and to help the ball to travel further and faster when struck.

Tom Box said Nixon "always was a dreamer", but the younger players promised to contact him when the tour ended in a month's time.

I was beginning to enjoy the company, and felt brave enough to ask a question which had been bothering me. I waited for a pause in the conversation, and then asked why a fifty-four-year-old man, like Old Clarke, would want to bowl fifty-seven overs, throughout the whole innings, when he had so many other bowlers in his team?

Well! I might as well have cracked a joke, because everyone burst out laughing!

"Why does a miser save his money, Mr. Umpire?" said Caffyn.

"He'd sooner meet his Maker than waste a shillin' on us poor boys!"

"He's the Devil, that's why, sir!" added Arnold, and the laughter started all over again. "Just ask Jemmy Dean, he'll be tellin' yer about that old pinchpenny!"

It had never occurred to me that Old Clarke would be able to pay bowlers less if they weren't called upon to bowl, but it seemed that this was his policy.

Joe had explained to me that there was lot of bad feeling towards Clarke ever since a bitter argument with two of his former players at Newmarket, last year, but I hadn't realised it was quite this bad!

Since then, the two men involved, John Wisden and Jemmy Dean, had founded "The United England Eleven" in direct opposition to Clarke, and were at this very moment playing a match in Bradford.

The hostility towards Clarke had become openly apparent at a meeting last September at the Adelphi Hotel in Sheffield, when fourteen of the leading professionals in England had signed a pledge "Never to play in a match for, or against, any eleven managed by William Clarke, because of the treatment they had received from him at Newmarket, and elsewhere."

George Anderson was renowned as a man with high morals and plenty of common sense, and he brought some calm to the conversation by telling me that there was truth on both sides of this argument.

After all, everyone here was still playing for Old Clarke, and could have joined the opposition if they had wanted to!

Although he was a Yorkshireman himself, he confessed that he would much sooner be staying alongside Torquay harbour tonight, than in the centre of Bradford! Once again,

George had been the voice of reason, and most of us nodded in agreement.

As George finished, Caesar got up and asked who wanted more beer, but before we had time to answer him the marquee flap opened and a coachman walked in.

"Beg pardon, sirs, but Mr. Clarke begs to inform you that your coach awaits."

It had been a good evening, but no one was sorry to be moving on now.

Joe knocked the tobacco from his pipe on to the grass, and everyone picked up their boxes. We said goodbye to the staff, and walked out into the twilight.

Most of the crowd had dispersed now, and the ground seemed strangely silent.

I hadn't told Joe that I was staying with Mr. John, just in case Old Clarke got the wrong ideas, but I waved to him as he hurried to join the others.

My pocket-watch told me that it was only 8.40, but I strolled up to the top gate anyway.

I sat down on the grass behind the oak tree, so that I couldn't be seen, and listened to the muffled sounds of music and laughter coming from the pavilion.

The top gate was open now, and a few minutes later, I heard the sound of a horse's hoofs approaching Chapel Hill Cross, and then the thudding as the wheels of a Hansom cab met the ruts and furrows of the outfield.

I peered around the tree, and watched it pull up outside the pavilion.

After about ten minutes, the pavilion door opened, and I saw a tall figure come out on to the balcony, surrounded by at least a dozen others. There was some hand shaking and some back slapping, before the man whom I assumed to be Mr. John skipped down the stairs to meet the coachman.

I came out from behind the tree, and, moments later, waved down the cab, and took the seat next to Mr. John.

"Welcome, my friend, and forgive me for condemning you to hide like a footpad!

The journey may shake up your bones, but there is a warm bed at the end of it."

The two lamps on the top of the cab gave enough light for the coachman to see the horse, and the horse had done this journey many times before. The noise of the wheels, and the clap of the hoofs ruled out a meaningful conversation, but it was good to be back alongside my old friend again.

After just under an hour, we passed over some high ground and I caught a glimpse of the sea. Soon after I did so, the cab turned off the road, and we were driving down an avenue of elm trees towards a pair of huge iron gates. Two men came rushing forward to open them for us, and tipped their caps as we passed through into the forecourt of a magnificent manor house.

"Welcome to Churston Court… the ancient seat of the Yarde family," said Mr. John, as we climbed out of the cab and headed towards the front door.

Once inside, we took off our boots, and Mr. John showed me through a narrow passage into the library.

The lanterns had been lit before we arrived, and Mr. John ushered me towards a leather-covered seat beside the fireplace.

He opened a cupboard behind me, brought out a jug of ale and two small glasses, and then sat down beside me.

For the next couple of hours, we discussed the day's play.

He asked me if I had noticed the Russian visitors, and then

told me that he had been asked to take a bat and ball to their tent to let them have a closer look.

Mr. John had been delighted by the size of the crowd today. There was no doubt now that Torquay could attract the sort of numbers which Teignbridge could only dream of.

Even though this year was Teignbridge's thirtieth Jubilee, Mr. John sensed that the club's best years were over unless it could compete with its seaside neighbour.

He then told me how disappointed he was that he had hired Cris Tinley.

Quite rightly, he had watched Tinley bowl tosses right into the bodies of two top professionals like Parr and Anderson, when Hillyer had so recently demonstrated just how helpful the pitch had become!

"Perchance, he is doing the bidding of that devil Clarke!" he said as he poured us another drink.

I asked him if the banquet was going well before he had to leave, and he nodded.

He said that there had been haunches of venison and lots of mutton, all washed down by jorums of punch and flagons of ale. When he left the pipes were being lit, and it was developing into an evening of toasts and singing.

Eventually, of course, the conversation turned to Old Clarke, and Mr. John told me that not one of the Devonshire batsmen knew how to play him.

He laughed and said, "The fox-headed old rogue bowled me twice at Teignbridge last year, and, on both occasions, the deliveries jumped up with a lot of screw on them!"

I felt sorry for Mr. John, but he was just one of many.

Old Clarke had taken nearly 400 wickets already this season, and had added another ten today!

When I was growing up, everyone bowled under-arm, and most of us learned to turn the ball both ways off the pitch. In time, of course, batsmen learned how to deal with that.

Then, eighteen years ago, after mounting pressure from those who wanted to bowl much faster, the rules were changed to allow round-arm bowling.

What no one had considered at the time was that a round-arm bowler can only turn the ball in one direction, and then, only in the same direction as the ball is travelling anyway!

The result is that now, in 1853, young batsmen never learn to bat against the turning ball, and of course in Old Clarke, they are facing the finest under-arm bowler that the world has ever seen.

Mr. John was nodding agreement as I spoke. Younger men like Vincent Tinley are now once again reverting to under-arm bowling, but lack the guile and the application of the fifty-four-year-old master!

We could have carried on talking all night but tomorrow would be another big day.

It was just after midnight when Mr. John led me down a long passage, and showed me into a room which he said was reserved for friends, and, in a few years' time, for a governess.

We shook hands, and he told me to meet him in the breakfast room tomorrow morning at six o'clock.

The wash-stand had been prepared for me, and I was pleased of the soap and water after a day outdoors.

It wasn't long before I stretched out on the bed, put my head on the feather pillow, and began to re-trace the details of what had been a remarkable day.

CHAPTER ELEVEN

The early morning sunlight came streaming in through my window, and woke me in time to dress for breakfast.

Molly had packed a clean shirt for me, but, otherwise, my coat and trousers seemed tidy enough to face another day.

When I arrived in the breakfast room, Mr. John was waiting for me.

The maid had laid out some cold ham and a jug of tea, and was just taking out some baked bread from the oven, when Charlotte arrived with two of the children.

"You are a most welcome guest," she said, as she offered me the back of her hand. "And I hope you rested well." I thanked her for her hospitality, and then bent forward to shake hands with the children.

"This is John, he's six years now, and this is Charlotte who is just four, aren't you, my dear?" Both children were beautifully dressed, and smiled back politely.

Mr. John added that little Louisa was still recovering from a fever, but seemed better this morning.

The maid put the hot bread on to the table, and added a second jug.

"Hot chocolate for madam, and for the children, as usual!" she said, and left us to chat over our breakfast.

I went over to the window and got my first view of the grounds of the house.

The lawns were carefully manicured, and already there was a gardener hard at work.

"I must compliment you on such a gracious home, milady," I said. "It has been a pleasure to be a guest here." Charlotte laughed, and explained that the whole house had been modernised in recent years to provide a suitable home for their growing family.

Mr. John's father, Sir John Yarde-Buller, the first Baron Churston, and his wife Elizabeth, lived in the much grander Lupton House which, she said, was just a few hundred yards away.

I remarked that it must take a lot of time to manage an estate like this, as well as to bring up three small children.

Charlotte smiled and nodded, and admitted that Mr. John helped her "when he's not off a-cricketing!"

Before Mr. John could plead his innocence, she added, "But I'll grant he's a better man than his great grandfather!"

They both laughed loudly, and then Charlotte explained that Mr. John's great grandfather was Judge Buller who became known as "Judge Thumb" after he directed that a man had the right to beat his wife, as long as the stick was no thicker than his thumb!

The two children enjoyed the story, and we were all still laughing when the maid knocked on the door to say that the coachman was ready to take us to Torquay.

I went back to my room to collect my bag and my box, said goodbye to Charlotte and the children, and walked out on to the courtyard to join Mr. John.

The cab looked much more impressive in the daylight, with its square frame, huge wooden wheels, and the four eagles of the family coat of arms on its polished woodwork.

Once he knew we were safely seated, the coachman took my luggage up on to his seat behind us. We saw the reins tense, then flick, and felt the first jerk forward that meant we were on our way, once again.

Mr. John leant over towards me and told me that he had asked the coachman to take us through Torquay on our way to Chapel Hill Cross, so that I could have a brief look at the rapidly expanding little town.

Here and there, it was a very bumpy ride, but we were early enough to miss most of the traffic.

We passed through the parishes of Paignton, and then Cockington, before we took a narrow lane down towards the sea.

In a few minutes we were driving along the sea-front, and I gasped at the view.

There was a British man-of-war anchored out in the distance, and, closer at hand, I caught a glimpse of the dark sails of two local trawlers, hard at work.

The road took us round to the town's harbour, with its quay and piers in front.

The harbour itself was surrounded on three sides by shops and the homes of the local tradesmen, whilst up on the hills behind it were tiers of tidy houses and elegant villas, some with marble fronts and terraces.

We passed the Hearder's Hotel, where the AEE were staying, and saw the Royal Hotel in the distance.

It was no surprise that this was becoming a very fashionable town to live in!

After finding our way through the heavy traffic on the harbour side, we headed back west, and Mr. John showed me the very different world of Swan Street, George Street, and Pimlico.

Here were narrow alleyways full of old houses and open sewers, and crowded by people who I guessed were domestic servants, or labourers, or perhaps even unemployed.

I had heard stories of the riots of just seven years ago, when crowds assembled in Lower Union Street, and burst into the bakery shops for food.

Several hundred "roughs" had swarmed down Fleet Street, attacking other shops, smashing shutters and windows as they went.

In the end, prisoners were taken and locked up in the Town Hall, until their fate came to the notice of sixty navvies working on the railway just outside Torquay, who marched to the Town Hall to free them.

As we drove up Lower Union Street, I could well imagine how these tragic events had come about!

However, we soon left the poverty of the lower town, and headed towards a suburb, which Mr. John told me was called Tor. The environment was much nicer here, and we found ourselves on a road edged by grassy verges and neatly trimmed hedges.

The road from the lower town was rising quite steeply now, and on the right we passed a handsome-looking church, which I was told was the new Upton Parish Church of St. Mary Magdalen.

It wasn't long before we had passed through Tor, and were heading out of the town towards Chapel Hill Cross.

On our way, we passed the railway station, where an excursion train had already off-loaded at least a hundred people, who were now carrying their bags towards the cricket ground.

They were spread across the narrow road, some being pushed into the hedge by tradesmen's carts, and others swearing as they were forced to give way to gig drivers heading for Newton Abbot.

Luckily, our coachman was content to bide his time, and, in due course, we turned off the road, climbed higher, and found ourselves looking down over the cricket ground once again.

I climbed out of the cab before we reached the top gate, thanked the coachman as he handed me my luggage, and then joined the long queue waiting for the gate to open. Mr. John gave me a wave, and the cab carried on towards the lower gate.

The sun was shining now, and everyone was smiling and chatting with each other as I gently pushed through to the front of the queue.

The policeman on the gate checked my M.C.C. registration, and I strolled down towards the pavilion.

I had noticed that the AEE coach had not yet arrived, so settled myself down on the steps of the pavilion to watch the tradesmen prepare their tents and booths for another busy day.

Mr. John had told me that Torquay Regatta was taking place today, so the crowd might be smaller than yesterday.

At the moment, there were long queues at both gates, and no sign that many had been tempted down to the waterfront.

Pearce was out in the middle with his mowing machine, so, to be friendly, I walked out to join him. From a distance I could see that several small mounds had developed overnight, so, as I passed them, I stamped them down as best I could.

"'Twill be winter time till them turfs behave, 'tis safe to assume sir!" he said.

"Or till you get a roller to be proud of!" I added, and he smiled and nodded.

He then told me that he had been called down to the ground at midnight, last night, to chase away several packs of dogs! It seemed that those who had bought an "Ordinary" from the food booths had left the meat bones in the long grass.

Whilst the club members were singing and dancing, most of the dogs in the neighbourhood had retrieved the bones, and were laying down on the pitch to enjoy them! When he arrived early this morning, there were still half a dozen dogs sniffing in the long grass.

I told him of the damage I had seen being caused by allowing spectators to roam across the pitch during the intervals, and asked if he had taken steps to prevent this happening today. To my relief he had seen the damage, and had agreed to pay some schoolboys to help him patrol the area during the lunch break.

Although it seemed an obvious requirement to me, I had to remember that this was the first time that either he, or this cricket club, had ever been involved in an occasion like this one.

Whilst we had been talking, the All England Eleven had arrived, both gates were now open, and the ground was filling up fast.

I had been carrying my bag and my hat box for over an hour now, so I made my way to the Eleven's marquee to put them away, and to find Joe.

When I got there, the flap was wide open to let in as much light as possible, and Joe was sat on a bench chatting with Tom Box.

"How was the hotel, my friends?" I asked.

"We could find no fault with it," replied Joe, and went on to tell me that he had enjoyed a walk around the harbour whilst the younger members were having a sing-song in the bar with the locals.

There was a big reading and news room in the hotel, where both he and Tom had been able to read the latest edition of *Bell's Life*, and the fifth edition of *Fred Lillywhite's Guide*, which had included all the details of the Eleven's matches in 1852.

The marquee was almost empty as most of the players had agreed to give Sam Parr and George Anderson some pre-match practice under the oak trees at the bottom of the ground.

There was still an hour before play was due to begin, so, perhaps inevitably, the conversation came round to the topic of the moment… M.C.C.'s 1839 change to the L.B.W. law, which had now fallen into utter disrepute.

Tom told me that most umpires were now refusing to consider any appeal from a round-arm bowler, on the grounds that it could not possibly be out!

The original law had stated that a batsman would be deemed to be out L.B.W. if the ball hit any part of his body *in a straight line from the bowler's hand to the striker's wicket, and would otherwise have hit it!*

The new law stated that the batsman would be out L.B.W. if the ball hit any part of his body *in a straight line from the bowler's wicket to the striker's wicket, and would otherwise have hit it.*

Considering that round-arm bowlers delivered the ball from at least three feet wide of the stumps, the result of the change had been that only under-arm bowlers could expect a decision in their favour.

Tom told us that Fuller Pilch, the leading batsman in England during the 1840s, was umpiring a match earlier this year, and the bowler had appealed for L.B.W.

Pilch had turned to him and said, "None of that, lad! Just bowl 'em out!"

Joe blamed the M.C.C. secretary, Roger Kynaston, who as a player had never bowled a ball in his life, and who, according to Joe "cared more for the sovereigns than for the statutes!"

After a while, the players drifted back to the marquee in pairs.

Sam Parr and George Anderson dragged their boxes towards the entrance flap, where we were sitting, and where there was some light to help them get ready to go out and bat.

George was a gentleman in a professional's disguise. His kit box was tidy and his shirts were neatly folded, with half a dozen collars pressed, and on studs beside them.

First, he strapped on his pads, and then added ties to top and bottom, to make sure that they stayed in place. Next, he picked out a right-hand glove which had strips of rubber running along the fingers and most of the thumb. Its palm had been cut away, but it was secured by a wrap-around strap. The left-hand glove had no rubber on its thumb, but the finger strips were longer with a U-shaped band to protect the first and fourth fingers. I was fascinated to see what the top professionals wore… we saw nothing like this at the garrison!

Just as I was thinking of leaving the marquee, I looked up and once again saw Old Clarke standing motionless in the entrance.

He was completely dressed in black, his tailcoat buttoned to the neck, and, of course, his top hat pulled down to just above his eyes.

He shouted to his son Alfred, who was joking and laughing with Julius Caesar, at the back of the marquee. Alfred heard him call, and came running past us. Father and son chatted for a moment before Alfred came back inside and asked us all to listen to what his father had just told him.

He told us that, because the marquee offered almost no view of the play, the Torquay Cricket Club had invited the All England Eleven players to watch the match from the pavilion balcony. Naturally, they wouldn't be allowed inside the pavilion itself, and, of course, lunch would be delivered to the marquee, but the club hoped that this gesture would appeal to the players.

A loud cheer followed the announcement, and, just for a moment, Old Clarke was a most popular captain!

In next to no time, the marquee emptied, and Joe and I soon followed.

As we walked through the crowd, it seemed just as busy as yesterday. We stepped on the grass, put on our top hats, and I walked over to see the scorers whilst Joe positioned the stumps.

The older scorer, a Mr. Pollard, passed me the Duke's ball which Mr. John had given him earlier.

I told him that the first over would be bowled from the bottom end, and then went out to join Joe.

As the twenty-two took the field, Joe pointed to some furrowing outside the right-hander's leg stump at the bottom end, and raised his eyebrows. I saw just what he meant, but it was too late to worry now!

Vincent Tinley once again opened the bowling from my end, and began with a couple of slow screwers from the leg side which Sam Parr allowed to pass by his off stump.

He hit the last ball of the over out towards Mr. Harris, who seemed to be talking to a passer-by near the fence. A shout from the crowd caught his attention, but he was too late to field it cleanly and the batsmen ran four whilst he searched for the ball in the long grass.

Next, Cris Tinley opened the bowling from the top end, and immediately pitched the ball up to George Anderson. Obviously, Mr. John had spoken to him, and he had taken the advice to heart.

After a couple of quiet overs, Anderson drove a ball straight past the bowler, and into the crowd behind. The crowd parted as the ball headed straight for one of the smaller beer tents.

The crowd shouted its usual response of "Booth Ball", and the batsmen set off on the first of what might be plenty of runs.

However, one of the younger men in the crowd had in fact fielded the ball before it entered the tent, hidden it, and then quietly passed it to Mr. Bere, the fielder!

Whilst the crowd kept up its chorus, the ball was thrown in hard, and the unsuspecting Sam Parr was run out by yards!

The crowd loved it! The young man raised his arms to acknowledge the cheers, and poor old Sam Parr walked back to the pavilion to the repeated sound of "Booth Ball! Booth Ball!" If the crowd was delighted to have seen the end of Sam Parr, it might have second thoughts now, as down the pavilion steps ran the athletic figure of the twenty-three-year-old Julius Caesar, from Godalming, in Surrey.

"Julie" to all his team-mates, was a dashing batsman who, at the moment, was trying to grow a Newgate fringe.

As he walked out to bat, I could see that, although he had shaved his upper and bottom lip, his side whiskers had not yet met under his chin, although he had done all he could with a brush to encourage them!

Julie was a highly-strung young man, and as he waited for Cris Tinley to come in to bowl, he tapped his bat nervously on the ground.

However anxious he may have appeared, he played Tinley's tosses and bouncers effortlessly, and the runs followed.

Vincent Tinley continued with his flattish screwers from my end, but was troubling neither batsman.

After another maiden over, Mr. John walked up to Vincent and asked him to give the ball more air so that "perchance these dullards might test our catching!"

Vincent snapped back, "Nay! I shan't sir. I shall gi'e him a good'un. If he wants to hit me, let him come and do it!"

Mr. John looked taken aback, and, before the next over, he threw the ball to Billy Buttress, and banished Vincent to the long grass at extra cover.

Because Billy was a round-arm bowler, he threw his deliveries higher into the air and gave them such a big screw that even the crowd could hear his fingers click as the ball left his hand. He grew his fingernails extra-long to enhance that effect.

After watching him bowl a few overs, I could see that he turned his screwer off his fourth finger, and from under his hand. The batsman had a choice of allowing it to pass by, or to use its bounce and try to hit it high over the fielders.

Although Billy was a likeable rogue, he wasn't very bright!

He regularly bowled his "other" delivery at the end of each over.

This time he bowled a straight ball at the batsman's leg stump, but flicked his *left* hand loudly to make him think it was another screwer!

He wasn't fooling today's batsmen, but every time he tried

the trick he would follow the ball down the pitch, grin at the batsman, and say, "Billy's a cunning cove!"

Compared with yesterday, the cricket was becoming dull.

George and Julie were two very stylish batsmen, and, knowing that they couldn't trust the pitch, relied mainly on defence.

With twenty-two fielders, and plenty of long grass against them, the batsmen were making slow progress.

Today, it was Joe who called time at two o'clock, and, as the two batsmen walked off undefeated, some elements in the crowd voiced their frustration.

The scorers told me that the total had reached 98 for just two wickets, although Fred Lillywhite in his printing tent was selling updated cards showing the score to be 99 for two!

I smiled, and assured them of my support, and left them still chattering about it!

In the distance, I could hear Pearce shouting at his team of boys saying, "Tell 'em to KEEP OFF!" I smiled at Joe, and we set off back to the marquee.

CHAPTER TWELVE

When we reached the marquee, the caterer's cart was blocking the entrance.

Most of the players were already inside and we watched them fighting over the drumsticks.

George Parr had managed to position eight of them between the fingers of both hands, and his friend Caesar was trying to dislodge them!

Most of the Eleven had spent the morning sitting politely on the pavilion balcony, so now some of them were relaxing with a bit of horse play.

The caterers had laid a long table today, and, in no time at all, we were all seated and washing down the meat with at least a dozen jugs of beer.

From the pavilion balcony, the players had had a close-up view of the young ladies under the oak tree, and several of them were comparing their virtues.

They were ribbing Tom Box, and Caesar shouted across the table,

"Which one's for you, Tom?" but Old Tom replied, "Her at home'll do for me, lad!"

As the shouting and joking grew louder, Joe and I found ourselves edging down the table towards Sam Parr and William Caffyn, where we could make ourselves heard.

Sam began the conversation by smiling and saying, "Forgive my young friend 'ere. He can't find any good words for our Lord and Master, that's for certain!"

William Caffyn had always disliked Old Clarke, and now that his son, Alfred, was larking around with the other youngsters, he could share his latest grievance.

Caffyn, as a twenty-five-year-old, had been asked to bowl just six overs in the Devonshire innings, whilst the forty-year-old Hillyer had been given fifty.

He knew only too well that Old Clarke would reflect that in the match fee, and unless he scored a fifty later today, he could expect another poor pay day!

Imitating Clarke's Nottinghamshire accent, he carried on to say, "Four pounds'll satisfy young William until he's got mouths to feed!" and then he added as an afterthought, "But I near forgot… the old devil's a miser, and now he's a pickpocket too! It'll end as three pounds and nineteen shillin's!"

Sam and Joe were both from Nottingham, and smiled at Caffyn's impersonation.

I gathered from listening that Old Clarke was now asking each of the players to contribute one shilling per match to cover his costs for "undertaking secretarial duties" for the Eleven. Joe smiled as if nothing surprised him anymore!

Time had passed quickly, and it was soon time for Joe and I to put on our top hats, and to find our way through the tents, and on to the ground once again.

Our arrival on to the outfield was the cue for the Subscription Band to strike up its first few notes, and this, in its turn, was the signal for the men in the crowd to leave the booths in droves, and to re-join their families on the grass.

Billy Buttress opened the bowling from my end, and was putting so much effort in to what he called his "bias" that he was almost falling over.

I reminded him that he had to have one foot behind the bowling crease in delivery, and he looked up at me, grinned, and said, "Yes! Muster M.C.C. sir!"

Perhaps if he had had more front teeth, the stench of ale would have been less overpowering!

Cris Tinley opened the bowling from the top end, and, immediately, worked up a much faster pace than earlier in the day. It seemed certain that Mr. John had asked for more effort, and that the young man was determined to produce it.

George Anderson was not easily rattled, but Tinley soon had him hopping about!

Several tosses, straight at his head, were followed by head-high bouncers.

During his first three overs, Joe had to call two wides and a bye, which flew past Mr. Hole before he could put a glove out to stop it.

It was all happening from the top end now, and the crowd were being treated to the fastest bowling they had ever seen.

Something had to give, and Tinley's fourth over provided it.

His first ball hit Anderson on the shoulder, and the second one pitched right into the furrow which Joe and I had noticed earlier.

Instead of bouncing, the ball shot along the ground and into Anderson's middle stump! George looked back at Tinley and grinned as he walked off.

As William Caffyn came in to replace him, I couldn't help but remember our lunchtime chat and secretly hoped that he might score the fifty which he had said he needed.

He began well, and cut Tinley's first ball towards the oak tree near the pavilion.

The ball hit the tree hard and bounced back towards The Honourable Mark Rolle who had chased it.

Predictably, the young ladies enjoyed the moment, and were still giggling amongst themselves as he threw the ball in to Mr. Hole, while the batsmen ran two.

The last ball of Tinley's over hit Caffyn's front pad, and the batsmen ran a single.

Joe's leg bye signal brought the expected loud laughter from the crowd, and two young men stepped out on to the outfield and performed a drunken type of country dance which involved smacking their thighs, and waving imaginary handkerchiefs. Two kindly stewards soon ushered them back with a smile.

All this time, Julius Caesar was batting comfortably. Only last week, he had scored 101 for the AEE against Kent, and now, as he played another of his favourite pull shots, clapping broke out from the pavilion balcony.

Soon, others who had been using their scorecards joined in, and, not long afterwards, the whole crowd was applauding his fifty. On this pitch it had been no mean achievement!

The score was mounting now, even though quite slowly.

Although Buttress was pitching his screwers on the stumps, both batsmen were simply allowing them to turn harmlessly by. He was varying his pace well, but the batsmen were content to wait for his loose ball.

One soon came along, and Caffyn was quick to cut it towards the fence, on the Chapel Hill side of the ground.

The two Surrey batsmen ran four whilst the crowd laughed at the sight of two children chasing their dog, then trying desperately to wrench the match ball from its mouth!

Although Buttress was proving ineffective, young Cris Tinley was still hurling the ball down from the top end, and two overs later, he bowled an over that would change the match.

Running in quickly, his first ball was a toss which hit Caffyn's front pad, and cannoned into his off stump. At lunch he had almost foretold his own future, and, now, as he walked off, William was facing the prospect of another £4 fee, less Old Clarke's shilling, of course!

Caffyn was on the pavilion balcony taking off his pads, before the next batsman came down the steps to join the fray.

Within moments, almost everyone in the crowd recognised George Parr, and there was a sort of reverential silence as he took his place at the wicket.

George was known as "The Lion of the North", and he looked every inch worthy of that title! Tall and muscular, George came from Nottingham, and was the son of a local farmer. No bowler ever intimidated George, least of all his Nottinghamshire colleague, Cris Tinley!

George settled into his crouching stance, and pushed Tinley's second ball into the off side for a single.

Despite Mr. John's advice, Tinley was bowling more tosses now, and his next ball was directed at Caesar's neck. It was very fast, and perhaps Julie should have ducked under it… but he didn't. Instead, he jumped up to try to defend it but could only watch it hit his shoulder and fall on to the bails.

The crowd was mesmerised by this sudden fall of wickets. Even Fred Lillywhite had left his printing tent to get a better view!

Two of England's finest batsmen dismissed in three balls... whatever next?

Tom Box was the next man in, at number seven, and from my position at square leg, I felt just a bit sorry for him. I had grown to like Tom, and wondered what he must be feeling as he waited to receive the last ball from a tearaway fast bowler who was less than half his age!

Flushed by his recent successes, Tinley chose to bowl another neck-high toss.

This time, Old Tom had guessed that it was coming, and pulled away to the leg side to avoid it. As it passed him, the ball clipped Tom's bottom glove, changed direction, and hit the wicket-keeper, Mr. Hole, flush on the nose!

As he fell, bleeding profusely, at least a dozen of the club members rushed from the pavilion.

Mr. John had been fielding at point, so was the first on the scene, whilst Joe and I kept well clear of the crowd which now surrounded him.

Mr. Hole was a founder member of the Torquay Club, and luckily he was still conscious and chatting to those who were trying to help him.

Once he knew that his wicket-keeper was not seriously hurt, Mr. John beckoned his fielders to him, and asked which of them would consider taking over behind the stumps.

I listened as, one by one, they came up with reasons why they were unsuited to the task! Finally, one said in a loud voice, "Doubtless one of our paid men would relish the task if it came with some extra tin!"

Mr. John called the three "given men" to him, and I heard him offer an extra five shillings to anyone who would take on the task. Although he had often done the job in the past,

THE MEADOW AT CHAPEL HILL CROSS

William Caffyn – J.C. Anderson – Lithograph of 1853

George Parr – J.C. Anderson – Lithograph of 1851

Vincent Tinley refused outright. Billy Buttress said he had never kept wicket before, and, as all eyes turned towards him, Cris Tinley must have realised that his fearsome bowling spell had just come to an abrupt end.

He took it all in good heart, and untied Mr. Hole's pads as the victim sat holding a cloth stemming the flow of blood from his nose.

Eventually, Joe and I ushered the well-wishers from the field while Mr. Hole got to his feet, and walked over to replace Cris Tinley at square leg, almost in front of the pavilion.

Billy Buttress bowled the next over from my end, and George Parr pulled his first ball straight out towards the recovering victim!

Mr. Hole had pulled out lumps of long grass, and was using them to wipe his face every time a new bleed occurred. Seeing the ball heading in his direction, he dropped the grass and dived full length to stop it. As he threw it back in, the crowd applauded him loudly, and he looked overcome by embarrassment.

At the end of Buttress's over, Mr. John called Vincent to replace his brother at the bottom end. The two seemed to have forgotten their earlier squabble, and Vincent asked for three more fielders to join Mr. Hole in the square leg area.

Mr. John looked surprised, but Vincent knew George Parr's strengths, and ended by saying, "George is a pretty hitter down square, sir, you'll be caused to thank me afore long!"

During the next few overs, Parr played both bowlers comfortably, and, time after time, pulled the ball square, for just a single, as Vincent had predicted.

George had been quite patient facing Buttress, but wasn't going to wait forever!

Suddenly, Billy bowled a shorter ball and George stepped across and hit it with all his considerable power.

The ball flew upwards, and straight over the thatched roof of the pavilion. The crowd gasped audibly, and about 2,000 people watched as it headed towards the row of oak trees on the western boundary.

Tom Box was not the fastest runner between the wickets, but the two batsmen set off to run as many as they could.

After they had run five, the loud call of "Lost ball" came from the pavilion, and I signalled to the scorers that I had awarded the statutory six runs because the ball could not be found.

A replacement old ball was thrown out, and sections of the crowd were still shouting "sixer, sixer" as George added a single, and faced Vincent's next over.

Although he didn't show it, George must have been caught up in the crowd's excitement, because he took a pace down the wicket to Vincent's first ball and tried to hit it over the fence on the Chapel Hill side of the ground.

This time, he was not so fortunate. The ball turned, beat the bat, and left Cris Tinley with a simple stumping.

The two brothers celebrated together, and as George walked off, I heard him muttering, "That ball had the very devil in her", and, from where I stood, I had to agree with him!

Replacing George was that wonderful cricketer of days gone by… Mr. Nicholas Felix.

Tom Box greeted him warmly as he reached the wicket, and every man, woman, and child in the ground today knew either of his scholarship, or of his legendary single wicket battles with Alfred Mynn.

As Vincent prepared to bowl, Mr. John stopped him and began to clap his hands.

"Left hand," he shouted, and after a moment of confusion, it slowly dawned on all twenty of the fielders that Mr. Felix was a left-hander. There are fewer than twenty left-handers playing in first-class cricket at the moment, and many of the fielders seemed unsure of where they should re-position themselves.

Most simply stayed where they were, and hoped they would get away with it!

Eventually, Vincent walked in, crouched down, and bowled a slow toss at Mr. Felix's midriff. Perhaps he hadn't expected it, but he took a pace back and hit it straight back at the bowler, who caught it easily.

Vincent had now taken two wickets in two balls, but that was the last thing on most people's minds as they watched the dejected figure of a former hero walk slowly back to the pavilion.

They say that when one life is lost, another is born, so perhaps there was an inevitability about this bright new cricket ground at Chapel Hill Cross becoming the final resting place of one of cricket's greatest champions.

Felix climbed the pavilion steps, accepted his team's commiserations, and, being an amateur, he was ushered into the heart of the pavilion to re-live his dismissal.

By the time I had finished watching Felix leave the field, Alfred Clarke had already reached the wicket to replace him.

Young Alfred was William's son, who, many believed, was being trained to take over the All England Eleven when his father finally retired.

He was only twenty-two but was already becoming a stylish, competent batsman.

Faced with the slow-medium pace of Buttress, and the slow under-arm of Vincent Tinley, it was never going to be easy for Tom Box and young Alfred to score quickly.

Neither was the type of batsman to be able to hit the ball high over the in-field, and the combination of the twenty-two fielders and the long grass was proving too much for them.

After half an hour, they had managed a few singles, and the crowd was becoming impatient.

Shouts of, "Come on, hit her, Tom!" were clearly audible now, and it all became too much for his patience.

Vincent bowled him a high looping lob, and Tom went down on one knee to try to pull it towards the pavilion. Sadly, he over-balanced and it clean bowled him.

Tom was always a popular figure with the spectators, and today they applauded him loudly as he made his way off.

The cheers turned to an awkward silence as William Clarke left the balcony, with his top hat pulled down over his eyes, and with a slight air of superiority in his stride.

Vincent's over had finished, and the next, from Buttress, proved uneventful.

As Joe and I passed each other in the middle of the pitch, we agreed that, according to our watches, the coming over would be the last of the day.

Old Clarke saw my signal to the scorers, and walked up for a chat with son Alfred.

I wondered what they were planning, and soon found out!

William hit Vincent Tinley's first ball out to cover point and called for an impossible single. Alfred got home easily, but William just walked to the bottom end, and was run out by half the length of the pitch.

William Hillyer was the last man to bat, and he walked out very slowly to join Alfred.

The batsmen had crossed, so Alfred faced Vincent's second

ball and pushed it for an easy single, leaving Hillyer to deal with the last two balls of the over.

As Vincent delivered the third ball, Hillyer recognised the screwer, and came running down the wicket to hit it hard, high, and straight.

The ball turned so sharply that it beat his bat, and the grasping gloves of stand-in wicket-keeper Cris Tinley, and somehow Hillyer survived.

Vincent was only a twenty-five-year-old, but he had been a professional for a few years now. He knew that Hillyer would attack the last ball of the day, and asked Mr. John to move fifteen men out to circle the edge of the ground, and to leave a point, a slip, a short leg, and two square legs all within ten yards of the bat.

Once the field was set, he walked up to the wicket, crouched down, and threw up a quick toss at Hillyer's chest. The batsman spun round to hit it square, but couldn't get on top of the ball and it went high in the air, and into the safe hands of Mr. Bere at short square leg.

Everyone seemed happy that the day had ended tidily, and that Devonshire would have the chance of setting the AEE a target tomorrow to ensure a good crowd on the third day.

As we walked off, Mr. John came over to me and asked if I could find alternative accommodation tonight.

He explained that Charles Hoare, whom he had known whilst at Oxford University, had asked to see Churston Court whilst he was in the area.

I told him that I had been privileged to be his guest last night, and that I was very happy to know that Mr. Hoare would be enjoying that honour tonight.

Joe had told me that the professionals had asked to leave

at 8.00 this evening, rather than at 9.00, so I was quite pleased to have a chance of an earlier night, if there was space for me on their coach.

CHAPTER THIRTEEN

The walk back to the marquee was no easier than yesterday.

At least a thousand people were still inside the ground, and most were showing no inclination to leave.

Joe and I had to push our way through families returning from the booths, either balancing plates of hot food or slurping drink from over-full jugs.

Fred Lillywhite was shouting out "Close of play score – just tuppence!" whilst his printing machine was clanking away in the background.

We passed a singer in ragged clothes offering his own version of "Farewell my Lilly dear" in exchange for a few coins in his cap, which he was swinging back and forth, in time with the chorus.

We were the first to get back to the marquee, so we thanked the young lad who had been paid to watch the entrance and he scampered off into the crowd.

As always, it was a pleasure to sit down after a long session and to put our top hats back into their boxes, before one of the younger players came in and sat on them.

Joe had been disappointed with the bowling of the "given men", the Tinley Brothers and Billy Buttress, and told me that he wasn't surprised that Old Clarke hadn't hired any of them for a while.

He said that if Cris Tinley's brain was as quick as his bowling, he might become a good professional, and dismissed the other two as being more interested in their pay than their performance!

I waited until his grumpy mood had passed before reminding him that, tomorrow, he would be umpiring William Clarke from the bottom end.

He seemed to have forgotten that umpires had to change ends after both teams had completed their first innings.

"Perchance the old rascal will overlook that, my friend," he said.

"He may overlook it, but for certain the Marylebone Club won't do so," I replied.

Joe was looking down at his boots now, and mumbled, "Then I will be as silent as the grave whatever tricks he plays!"

Both of us knew that Clarke would be after a quick end to play tomorrow, and that he might try anything to ensure that he collected his money, and made an early getaway.

If one of Joe's decisions upset his plans, he knew that he wouldn't be playing at Islington on Friday! Little wonder that Joe would opt for silence!

By now, the caterers were laying the tables and the younger lads were laughing and fooling about, after spending most of the day sat doing nothing in the sun.

Only George Anderson and Tom Box were seated at the table, chatting together, whilst William Caffyn was still sulking in the far corner.

Food has a way of changing the atmosphere, and it wasn't long before we were all sat at the table eating.

Caesar was pouring beer from a jug, and Cris Tinley was annoying a waitress by untying her apron every time she walked past.

The main topic of conversation was the news that Alfred Clarke had been down to the station, and booked tickets for a cheap four o'clock excursion train tomorrow afternoon to take the AEE players to London for Friday's match in Islington.

Alfred did most of the travel organisation for the Eleven, and it seemed that the owner of the coach had more lucrative work to do in Cornwall.

Joe told me that Old Clarke had probably booked cheap accommodation in London, and that because the train wouldn't arrive until late, the players wouldn't notice if the hotel was a bit seedy!

The big talking point was the assumption that the Eleven could take twenty-one wickets much sooner than they had done yesterday! Old Clarke must have been confident, but not all the players saw it his way, even if Hillyer was fit to bowl!

George Anderson was still chatting serious stuff with Tom Box, and I could hear their conversation moving from the prospects of imminent war in the East, to the news that the U.S.A. was playing an international cricket match against Canada.

As the tables were being cleared, George Parr was ordering his favourite gin and water, and his horse-play with Julius Caesar was getting rowdier by the minute.

"Julie", who knew London well, was promising to take George to the Eagle Tavern in City Road on Friday night, and Billy Buttress was doing eagle impressions to annoy them both.

A minor scrap broke out between the three of them, but it came to nothing, and at least some surplus energy was spent.

Just as the caterers began to clear the table, Old Clarke put his head around the entrance to the marquee, and beckoned us all to follow him.

Hoping that there would be room to take me with them, I picked up my box and bag and took a quick cut to the area behind the pavilion where the horses had been stabled for most of the day. The coachman was waiting beside the coach, and seemed pleased of some company.

He told me that he had spent most of the day trying to keep his horses cool, and "away from them Lucifer's leaves" which I found out later referred to the leaves of some yew trees on the border of the ground, which are poisonous to horses.

Before long, everyone had arrived and passed their boxes to the coachman.

Whilst he was securing them, I climbed in with the others, and young Cris Tinley sat on the floor between our feet.

Luckily, Mr. Felix was staying for the soiree in the pavilion, so although it was a squash, there was just enough room for an umpire, without his top hat!

A crack of the whip and a shout from the coachman saw us on the move, and as we left by the bottom gate, I caught a glimpse of Pearce still sweeping the pitch.

Fifteen minutes later, the coach pulled up behind a queue of cabs outside the Hearder's Hotel, and as we got out on to Victoria Parade I could see that the whole harbour area was packed with people.

I wanted cheaper accommodation than the hotel, so, as most of the players took their boxes straight to their rooms, Joe stayed behind to help me.

He had met the proprietor, Mrs Sarah Hearder, yesterday and asked one of the staff to call her.

After a few minutes, a lady in a tight corset and an embroidered skirt was walking across the entrance hall to meet us.

Joe introduced me as "an officer with the Marylebone Club" and the lady seemed suitably impressed.

I explained that I just needed a small room, nearby, for one night, and she thought for a moment before asking us to follow her to the main entrance.

She led us around the side of the hotel, and then pointed to a tall terrace of houses on the other side of the harbour.

"That's Vaughan Parade, sir, and you will locate Ellen Mudge in the endmost property, and tell her Mrs. Hearder directed you."

I thanked her for her advice, and she replied, "You'll find no fault in Miss Ellen, sir."

After she had left us, I turned to Joe, shook his hand, and arranged to meet him outside his hotel at nine o'clock tomorrow morning.

As I strolled round the harbour, the light was fading fast. Fishermen were shouting to each other as they prepared their boats for another night along the south coast, and mothers were dragging their children home before it got dark.

As Mrs. Hearder had predicted, Ellen had one room free in her lodging house, and luckily it overlooked the harbour.

As she showed me up the staircase, and along a number of dark, narrow corridors, I wondered how I was going to find my way back to the door again tomorrow!

Eventually, we reached my room, and although very small it had a comfy-looking bed, a chair, a wash-basin full of water and two new towels.

I told Ellen that the room would suit nicely, and paid her with a small tip.

It had been a long time since waking up at Churston Court this morning, so I was pleased to put down my bag and box, and to close the window before stretching out on the bed.

In just two days, I had so much to tell Molly. She wouldn't believe that I had spent a night in a manor house, and was now laying here alongside Torquay harbour.

Even without the cricket, it had been a huge adventure, and so far I had loved every moment of it.

Captain Rush would want to know every tiny detail of the past two days… but I wondered where he was now. Was his regiment still in England? Was he on his way to Turkey? Was he still alive?

I shuddered as I considered each possibility but then decided that at the moment there was no war, so what was the point of worrying in advance?

*

In the morning, I was woken by the sounds of the harbour and the warmth of the early morning sun through the window.

By eight o'clock, I had washed and dressed, and was finding my way out of Miss Ellen's lodging house to begin another exciting day.

I decided to have a stroll up the hill behind the harbour, and ended up in a very pretty area called Torwood Gardens.

I found my way through the cast-iron fencing which surrounded the area, and sat down on a bench to admire the display of late summer colour. There was a stream running past, and already a man was tending to the beds of sunflowers and marigolds just a bit higher up the hill.

It was a lovely peaceful place, yet so close to the bustle of the town centre, and I thought how much Molly would have enjoyed it.

After a while, I made my way back down the hill to the harbour, and stood watching the frenzied activity of those who made their living there.

I noticed half a dozen men on the slipway, shouting and pulling desperately on a rope, so I ran down to offer my help.

A boat had broken free from its moorings, and they were trying to secure the rope to a ring on the harbour wall.

A couple more men soon joined and we got enough rope through the ring to tie it. At one point, my top hat box almost rolled into the water, but I saved it just in time!

Once the boat was secure, the man who seemed to be in charge thanked me for helping and called out to a young lad, "Take my friend to see Samuel." I followed the youngster who led me to a man cooking fish on a gridiron.

"Jack sent 'im," the lad said, and ran off.

Samuel obviously knew what was meant, and handed me some bread, and a spatula full of small pale-coloured fish from the grate. I sat down on a low wall and enjoyed every mouthful!

Time was passing now, so I walked around to the Hearder's Hotel, where the coach was already waiting.

I greeted the coachman, and went to climb inside. As I opened the door, I saw that on the floor, he had left his blanket and a straw-filled pillow.

I gathered them together, and handed them up to him.

"I trust you slept well, my friend," I said.

"Too much commotion for that 'ere, sir!" he replied.

It wasn't long before the players were climbing into the coach.

I had offered to sit up on top, with the coachman, but was told that William Hillyer had already requested that seat.

When not on the field, William spent most of his time keeping away from the others, just in case someone trod on his toes! He was safer up with the coachman!

It was a tight squash inside the coach, but a lot better than walking!

Sarah Hearder and some of her staff came out to wave the coach goodbye, and we left this quaint little harbour for the last time.

CHAPTER FOURTEEN

After the short journey from the harbour, we arrived at Chapel Hill Cross and drove in by the bottom gate.

It was soon clear that there were not so many traders here today, but there were still long queues at both entrances.

The coach stopped outside the marquee to let us climb out, before heading off towards the oaks behind the pavilion.

Although Old Clarke had arrived early, and opened the marquee for us, he was now back in his own tent where he had much work to do.

Today was his pay-day, so he had invoices to write and decisions to make.

Joe had told me that once he had decided just how much to pay each member of the Eleven, he would call his son Alfred to record the amounts in his accounts book, and to write a receipt for the cricket club.

Back in the marquee, there was plenty of speculation about how much each member would receive. Most were quietly pessimistic, whilst others were threatening to "go to Jemmy" (James Dean was one of the founders of the United England Eleven) next season if they were underpaid.

Charles Arnold and William Caffyn were not expecting to bowl today, now that Hillyer was semi-fit again.

Both knew that Old Clarke would limit his bowlers to as few as he could, so that he could pay the rest just for batting!

Loud voices from outside meant that the gates had now been opened, so it was time for Joe and I to leave the marquee and to carry out the pre-match formalities whilst there was still plenty of time.

One of the scorers was already seated at his table, and he threw us the new match ball.

The noisy camaraderie of the Devonshire players filled the air as they gathered on the pavilion balcony chatting and laughing with the club members.

Just as I was feeling relaxed about the prospects of an interesting last day's cricket, Joe called me urgently to the bottom end of the pitch where he was checking the size of the stumps. As I approached, I knew what he was going to say… the whole area from six feet in front of the popping crease to six feet behind the stumps had been saturated with water.

Whatever had happened? I told Joe that I would go to find Pearce and ask him to explain.

Five minutes later, I found Pearce in his little room under the pavilion balcony.

He could tell that I was worried, and began to blurt out the story.

It seemed that, after we left last night, a young man arrived for the soiree in a private carriage.

Something spooked his horse, and it bolted towards the pitch.

Pearce was working on the top end, saw the horse coming, and shooed it away.

As it turned back towards the pavilion, it dragged the carriage's wheels sideways, and completely removed a square foot of turf from just in front of the leg stump at the bottom end.

Pearce explained that he had cut a piece from the outfield, and trimmed it to fit into the bare patch left by the accident.

He had worked until dark to repair the damage.

Because the pitch was so dry, he had to soak the area to be able to stamp the new turf into place. He said that he had done a similar repair job when he was working at Windmill Hill, and that the match had carried on without further incident.

From anywhere on the playing area, the new turf was very obvious.

It was clear that Pearce had done his best, but if Hillyer was bowling from the top end again, he would be hitting that new turf with every ball he bowled!

Before long the two captains, Mr. John and Old Clarke, joined us out in the middle, and the crowd was beginning to get excited. Clarke spotted the patch immediately and bent down to examine it. I couldn't see his face, but he was probably licking his lips!

Guessing that the crowd would be smaller today, Mr. John had asked Pearce to extend the mown area on the Chapel Cross side to allow the ball to travel further before meeting the long grass, and Clarke had raised no objection.

It struck me that his time would have been better spent preparing a new pitch, but it was too late to worry now.

One by one, the All England Eleven had joined William Clarke out in the middle. Now that the crowd had become used to seeing the likes of George Parr and Nicholas Felix in the flesh, the cheers were being replaced here and there by some unpleasant name-calling.

At eleven o'clock, Mr. Beckley and Mr. Kitson, both wearing their boaters, left the pavilion to the familiar reception from the ladies, who had taken up their usual place under the oak tree.

I nodded to the scorers, handed the new ball to Clarke, and took up my place behind the stumps at the top end.

To my complete surprise, and no doubt to Joe's huge relief, Clarke had decided to bowl from my end once again, though this time down the slope!

As he bent down and rubbed the ball in the dirt, I suddenly realised that he must have chosen to bowl into the new patch, even if it was against the slight slope.

The more experienced Mr. Kitson had opted to take the strike, and watched carefully as Clarke trotted in and delivered from under his armpit.

The ball pitched on the new turf and shot along the ground to hit the middle stump!

Clarke had followed up halfway down the wicket, and called out, "That's two ciphers for you sir, if I'm not mistaken!" Mr. Kitson didn't bother to answer him.

The crowd gasped as they realised that a wicket had fallen after just one ball, but worse was to follow when Mr. Mordecai Collier was dismissed by the third one too!

Clarke hit the patch again but this time the ball jumped up, clipped the batsman's glove, and lobbed up to George Parr who had been positioned at point for that exact delivery.

Young Mr. Beckley had watched all this going on from the other end, but now it was his turn to face William Hillyer.

"Topper" was a quiet fellow, but as I watched him shuffling in to begin his spell, I wondered what he must have thought when Clarke stole the best end from him.

But then again, maybe it wouldn't have been so helpful to a round-arm bowler who tended to pitch *outside* leg stump and to send the ball across the batsman.

Whatever he felt, he wasn't showing it, and his first over was as accurate as ever.

Mr. Beckley hit the second delivery out towards Mr. Felix, took the chance to run two and the innings was underway.

The new batsman, Mr. Compton, had swaggered to the wicket, smiling and laughing with the fielders as he did so.

His happy-go-lucky style had proved effective in the first innings, and the crowd hadn't forgotten his big hit into the beer tent which had yielded eight runs.

As Clarke came in to begin his second over, the crowd had already begun to chant "Booth Ball! Booth Ball!"

I watched Clarke's hand as he threw up a high screwer which pitched six inches outside Mr. Compton's leg stump. The batsman tried to club it towards long-on but the ball turned sharply from the drying pitch, and took his off stump.

Clarke resisted making a remark this time. Perhaps he sensed that Mr. Compton might be bold enough to return it with interest!

Three wickets had now fallen for just two runs and Devonshire needed an experienced man like Mr. Hounsell to come in and steady the ship.

He saw out the rest of Clarke's over, and his partnership with Mr. Beckley began to flourish.

Runs were very slow in coming, and when they did, they came in singles.

Clarke appealed for LBW after an screwer had hit Mr. Beckley in front of his stumps, but it had clearly pitched outside off stump, and the current law states that the ball must have pitched in a straight line between wicket and wicket.

Hillyer appealed for a catch by Tom Box, but Joe ruled that the snick, which was audible to us all, had hit Mr. Hounsell's brass belt buckle, not his bat.

Clarke was making every ball turn from off the new patch and it wasn't long before Mr. Beckley was bowled by one which kept very low.

Billy Buttress was the first of the three professionals to bat, and as he walked in, Mr. Hounsell met him for a short chat.

In the first innings Buttress had called for a silly run, and Mr. Hounsell didn't want to be run out by yards this time!

He needn't have worried because, next over, Billy was caught at point by George Parr as he fended off a high bouncing delivery from Hillyer.

"Topper" was enjoying bowling from the bottom end, and he was accurate enough to be able to hit one of the ridges which had formed outside the leg stump.

Cris Tinley had pushed a couple of singles towards the pavilion before he became Hillyer's next victim, and was caught at slip by Samuel Parr.

It was not the ideal time for an apprentice professional to show his worth, and I felt sorry for young Brown as he marked his spot in front of the batting crease.

He had stood at my end whilst Clarke had bowled a maiden over to a very careful Mr. Hounsell, but now had to face up to Hillyer himself.

He watched the first ball go harmlessly by, but then played a forward defensive to the second delivery. He didn't get quite to the pitch, and the ball leapt up, struck his glove, and gave George Parr his sixth catch of the match, at point.

As Brown walked off, he looked dejected and I wondered

if his match total of six runs would get him his contract with Torquay Cricket Club, and, furthermore, just how many he might have scored on a better pitch than this one!

Even though wickets were falling regularly now, Old Clarke was getting very impatient with Mr. Hounsell. Clarke had tried almost every different ball in his repertoire, but, each time, Mr. Hounsell had simply stepped forward and defended it.

This time, Clarke began by offering a gentle toss from under his hand, only to watch the batsman play forward once again. As he followed through down the wicket, Clarke shouted, "Does she frighten you, sir?"

His second ball was quicker but met the same fate, and another insult followed.

Clarke delivered his third ball from right up under his armpit, with the same faster action as before, but this time the ball seemed to slow dramatically as it left his hand, Mr. Hounsell was completely fooled and fell forward.

A slight smile flicked across Clarke's face, as it just missed the stumps.

I was as surprised as the batsman, and glanced at Joe, who had turned his head away as though disowning the moment.

My first thought was that Clarke had retained his usual right-handed bowling action, but had delivered the ball from his left hand instead. Anything was possible with this rascal, but surely that was beyond even him!

As he bowled the last ball, I watched his bowling hand carefully but, this time, he ended his over with a straightforward screwer into Mr. Hounsell's pads.

In the meantime, Mr. Charles Hoare had replaced Brown, and had watched Clarke's over with interest.

Devonshire needed a sizeable contribution from Mr.

Hoare, and he began confidently by clipping a bouncer from Hillyer over Tom Box, and into the long grass. It took a while for the fielder to find it, and the batsmen ran four.

At last, the crowd had something to cheer, and Mr. Hoare tipped his boater in acknowledgement.

At the end of Hillyer's over, Clarke walked back to his bowling mark, sat down on the grass, and made a yawning gesture with the flat of his hand.

The crowd enjoyed his humour, and even more so when he walked down the pitch, faced Mr. Hounsell, and posed in a forward defensive mode.

I felt so sorry for Mr. Hounsell who stood silently looking down at his boots.

At last, the over got underway, and Clarke threw up a gentle lob as if bowling to a child, and Mr. Hounsell played forward defensively, once again.

Clarke was cursing under his breath now, and his second ball was a quick one, delivered from high under his armpit, but it met the same fate.

I wondered what he would try next, so took a pace back, and watched him use the same fast arm action as before, but deliver a ball which just floated slowly towards the batsman.

Just as in the last over, Mr. Hounsell was fooled, and began to fall forward as I shouted, "No ball!"

This time, by taking a step back, I had spotted just what Clarke was up to!

The crowd hushed, and every fielder was watching me as I signalled to the scorer.

Clarke turned round and stared at me. His glass eye and long nose made him seem even more sinister than I had ever noticed before.

In the heat of the moment, I managed to stay calm, and explained to Clarke that I had seen him snag his elbow against his ribs, in delivery, instead of allowing his arm to swing freely through the action.

According to the Laws of Cricket, this constituted a "jerk", and, as he had now offended twice, I had no-balled him.

Clarke turned to his team-mates, and opened his arms in apparent disbelief.

By now, we were in the middle of the pitch, and I called Joe to join us.

Since he had offended twice, I told Clarke to hold out his right arm so that I could "chalk" him.

"What the dooce?!" he shouted, and spat on the grass in front of me.

Quietly, I told him that either he allowed me to chalk him, or the game would end, and I would report his actions to the Marylebone Club.

Only a few in the crowd understood what I was doing, but the word spread fast, and jeering and laughter soon followed.

Clarke raised his right arm, and I took the chalk from my pocket and spread it thickly on to the inside of the elbow area of the sleeve of his grey shirt.

Clarke's personal pride was very important to him, but nothing was as important as his livelihood, and only the Marylebone Club could threaten that!

When eventually play was resumed, Mr. Hounsell pushed a single off the last ball.

I called "Over" and asked Clarke to lift his arm to confirm that the chalk was undisturbed. As he walked out to extra cover, he was met by a group of young men, dancing towards him with their right arms extended. I tried not to smile!

It was Hillyer's turn to bowl now, and once again he was proving lethal from the bottom end.

His first ball was a fast toss which angled in at leg stump, and bowled Mr. Hounsell behind his legs. Although he had not scored many, his had been a brave innings!

It was now obvious that Hillyer was becoming harder to play as the pitch deteriorated.

To those who had never faced him, his slim frame, his top hat, and his gentle medium pace seemed to carry very little threat.

But, although now forty years old, he knew exactly what to do on a surface which gave his deliveries such an uneven bounce.

His round-arm action meant that the ball was pitching six to nine inches outside the batsman's leg stump and was either going across him, or behind his legs.

Most amateur batsmen use a stance in which their bat is grounded six inches wide of the toes of their boots.

If a right-handed batsman chooses a stance on his leg stump, he will expose his off stump, and is liable to edge a drive into the slips.

If he chooses a stance on middle stump, he will expose his leg stump, and have to play most shots from around his pads.

In practice, most of the Devonshire batsmen chose to just wait and see, and then fell victim to the varying bounce.

Mr. Hole managed a couple of runs before being bowled by one which hit the bottom of his off stump, whilst Vincent Tinley went for a big drive, missed the ball, and was easily stumped by Tom Box.

At the other end, Clarke was now concentrating on hitting the drying patch as often as he could, and for him, that meant three times out of four.

Clarke never forgot a batsman's weakness, and bowled Captain Fyfe with an screwer from outside off stump,, just as he had in the first innings.

The Honourable Mark Rolle, in his Eton cap, came in at number thirteen and was soon facing Clarke, who couldn't resist a remark to unsettle him.

As he trotted in to bowl, he shouted, "Mind your bat, not your bonnet, this time sir!"

The seventeen-year-old looked nervous, and played forward to a ball which turned six inches and took his off stump.

"Oooh! We've 'ad another haccident if I'm not mistaken sir!" said Clarke as the lad walked off with his second "duck's egg" of the match.

Luckily, he didn't seem to take his failure to heart, and, after he had walked off, he went to sit with the young ladies under the oak tree, who now had something much more interesting than cricket to concentrate upon.

All this time, Mr. Hoare was batting carefully, and adding a single whenever one came his way.

Mr. Bere came in to join him, and had decided that a robust approach was what was needed in these circumstances.

He came down the wicket to hit a faster ball from Clarke high on the leg side for two useful runs, but only managed it once!

Guessing that Mr. Bere would try to repeat the shot, Clarke produced a delivery which Joe had told me about, but which I had never seen before.

Just like the previous ball, Clarke delivered it from high under his armpit, but, this time, just before releasing it, he allowed the ball to roll up his hand so that he could push it forward with his wrist.

Mr. Bere ran forward but, this time, the ball just looped slowly up into the air.

The change of pace had fooled him, and he slipped as he tried to hit it with all his might. As he fell on to his backside, the ball arrived, and rolled slowly on to his middle stump.

If Mr. Bere was embarrassed as he picked himself up, the crowd enjoyed his predicament and, as he walked off, it roared its approval of Clarke's cunning.

By now, the Devonshire players had realised that they were not going to save this match, so, one after another, they decided to chance their arms, and go down like gentlemen.

Mr. Gully called for a silly single and ran out Mr. Hoare by over a yard.

Then he himself managed a couple of hearty blows before losing his wicket to Hillyer.

Mr. Martin came in and kept one end going, but was soon running out of partners.

Captain Mills was caught by Sam Parr, at extra cover, off Clarke, and Mr. Coleridge was run out trying to turn a three into a four.

Neither Mr. Harris, nor the Torquay Cricket Club captain, Mr. Julian, added to the scoreboard before both fell to balls from Hillyer which took their leg stumps.

I felt sorry for Mr. Julian who had been bowled for nought in both innings, in front of his own home crowd.

He tried to avoid looking at the spectators as he made his way back to the pavilion.

Despite the activity of the last twenty minutes, I made certain that I checked Clarke's elbow at the end of each over, and now he was cooperating willingly.

Mr. John gave me a smile as he joined Mr. Martin at the

At Torquay, in Devonshire, August 22, 23, and 24, 1853.

Twenty-two of Devonshire.	1st Inn.	2nd Inn.	
H. Beckley, Esq., c G. Parr, b Hillyer	1	b W. Clarke	6
J. Kitson, Esq., c G. Parr, b Hillyer	0	b W. Clarke	0
M. Collier, Esq., c G. Parr, b W. Clarke	5	c G. Parr, b W. Clarke	0
F. Compton, Esq., c Anderson, b Hillyer	16	b W. Clarke	
W. Hounsell, Esq., run out	4	b Hillyer	6
W. Buttress, c A. Clarke, b W. Clarke	1	c G. Parr, b Hillyer	0
R. C. Tinley, c Box, b Hillyer	8	c S. Parr, b Hillyer	2
J. Brown, b W. Clarke	6	c G. Parr, b Hillyer	0
C. H. Hoare, Esq., st Box, b Hillyer	10	run out	8
Captain Fyfe, b W. Clarke	26	b W. Clarke	2
W. Hole, Esq., c Anderson, b W. Clarke	5	b Hillyer	2
Vincent Tinley, b Hillyer	4	st Box, b Hillyer	0
Hon. M. Rolle, st Box, b Hillyer	0	b W. Clarke	0
M. Bere, Esq., b W. Clarke	6	b W. Clarke	2
C. Gully, Esq., b W. Clarke	3	b Hillyer	4
G. Martin, Esq., c A. Clarke, b W. Clarke	4	b Hillyer	11
Captain Mills, b Caffyn	0	c S. Parr, b W. Clarke	5
W. Coleridge, Esq., run out	0	run out	3
G. Harris, Esq., b W. Clarke	2	b Hillyer	0
— Julien, Esq., b Caffyn	0	b Hillyer	0
J. Yarde Buller, Esq., not out	0	not out	0
J. Collier, Esq., b W. Clarke	0	b Hillyer	2
Byes 3, leg byes 2	5	Byes 0, wides 0, noes 1	1
	106		54

Bowlers.	Balls.	Runs.	M.O.	Bowlers.	Balls.	Runs.	M.O.
W. Clarke	228	49	32	W. Clarke	116	34	15
Hillyer	200	48	25	Hillyer	115	19	17
Caffyn	24	4	4				

The England Eleven.	1st Inn.
S. Parr, run out	11
C. Arnold, c Kitson, b V. Tinley	9
G. Anderson, b R. C. Tinley	42
Julius Cæsar, b R. C. Tinley	57
W. Caffyn, b R. C. Tinley	6
G. Parr, st R. C. Tinley, b V. Tinley	18
T. Box, b V. Tinley	18
N. Felix, Esq., c and b V. Tinley	0
A. Clarke, not out	3
W. Clarke, run out	0
W. Hillyer, c Bere, b V. Tinley	0
Byes 4, leg bye 1, wides 3	8
	172

Bowlers.	Balls.	Runs.	M.O.
Buttress	88	35	6
V. Tinley	154	56	13
R. Tinley	188	73	17

England winning in one innings and 12 runs.

All England Eleven v. 22 of Devonshire at Torquay in 1853

Alfred Mynn (left) and Nicholas Felix (right)

crease, and was relieved, no doubt, to have avoided facing Clarke for at least a few more balls.

It was Mr. Martin who had that task, and he set about it energetically.

He pulled the first ball into the long grass near the top entrance, and ran four.

Two more were added from the third ball, and he ran a single off the last one.

It was a brave gesture, and the crowd appreciated it, but now it brought him up to the top end to face Hillyer coming up the slope.

He had survived by playing Hillyer very carefully, but now, with only the tail to bat with, he knew that he had to attack him.

He tried to drive the first ball of the over, but Hillyer hit a ridge, and the ball shot along the ground to knock over his off stump.

The crowd applauded him loudly as he made his way back to the pavilion, and Mr. John whispered to me that Mr. Martin was the only batsman to have reached double figures!

His departure seemed to be the signal for large sections of the crowd to stand up, and make their way towards the food and drinks tents.

This didn't appear to worry Mr. John Collier, who strode in to bat with a broad smile on his face.

No one doubted what was in his mind, and he soon proved them right.

Hillyer's second ball leapt up past his shoulder, and Mr. Collier got nowhere near it… but it was just a temporary reprieve.

"Topper" knew just what to do next, and took his middle stump with a toss.

I signalled to the scorers, nodded to Joe, and removed the stumps for the last time.

Twenty-one wickets had fallen in little more than two-and-a-half hours.

CHAPTER FIFTEEN

As we walked off, Mr. John shook my hand, and thanked me for umpiring.

I reminded him that he had batted in both innings but not faced a single ball!

He smiled and, as he left to go up the pavilion steps, he called out to me that at least it was an improvement on last year at Teignbridge, where he had been out twice for just one run!

I walked over to thank the scorers, Mr. Pollard and Mr. Curtis, and to confirm that there were no outstanding issues that needed mentioning in my match report.

When I got there, I found Joe was already chatting with them.

Most of the crowd had decided to have lunch early, and to enjoy a day out, as long as there was plenty to eat and drink. To many, the cricket was just a necessary distraction anyway!

When we got back to the marquee, the caterers had not anticipated the early finish and were trying to lay the table with whatever they could find that could be prepared quickly.

It meant that the choice was restricted to plates of bread, pickles, cheese, cucumbers, and of course jugs of beer.

From the moment we pulled back the flap of the tent, almost everyone came towards us, and congratulated me for chalking Old Clarke.

I was quite a hero, and even Joe admitted that he wouldn't have dared to do it!

"The old rogue's a cheat, and has always been so!" said Caffyn, and most of his mates nodded in support.

Old Tom Box added, "He'll likely chalk his pockets now to mind we don't steal his money!"

Just as everyone was adding their own sentiments about their captain, his son, young Alfred, came in through the flap.

He told us that he had just come from his father's tent, and that William was now asking to see everyone, but strictly one at a time.

Everyone knew that this was the way in which Old Clarke liked to reward his players, and, because he had the reputation for being a miser, no one wanted to go first!

The theory was that he would start by being extra careful in the amounts he was paying out, but then, as he reached the last few, he would realise that he had more coins left than he had expected, so would end up by being more generous!

In the end, it was decided that Julius Caesar should go first, because Clarke couldn't afford to be mean towards one of his major attractions.

As we carried on eating our lunch, Joe explained to me that Old Clarke usually paid the players between £4 and £6, depending on their reputations, with extra for any travelling costs which they may have incurred... at least, that was the way it was supposed to happen, but you never knew with Clarke!

"Julie" came back smiling, but didn't tell us how much he had been paid. He just told us that Clarke was sitting in front of a small table, with little piles of various coins in front of him, and that "I'll vow none of us will go short today!"

One by one, the players left the marquee to collect their match fees, and most returned looking fairly happy.

With the United England Eleven searching for next season's recruits, Clarke could not afford to be too mean, and, today, it seemed as if he understood that.

Joe came back with £4, which was all he had expected as an umpire, and we were the last to leave the lunch table.

Suddenly, the marquee had become a hive of activity as the caterers were clearing the dishes, and taking the table tops off the trestles. Most of the players were packing their boxes, and were shouting to make themselves heard.

Bats had been mislaid, and gloves borrowed but not returned.

Some of the lads had changed into new pairs of trousers, and smooth-soled boots, while others were happy to travel in their match kit.

As they made their way out of the marquee for the last time, the younger ones were comfortable in shirt and neckerchief while the older players favoured an ordinary morning tailcoat, usually buttoned at the neck.

Whilst we had been in the marquee, the crowd had gathered around the pavilion to catch a last glimpse of the players and to hear the post-match speeches.

The Torquay Cricket Club chairman, Mr. Cary, with club secretary William Kitson by his side, began by thanking the All England Eleven for being "capital fellows" throughout, and for attracting a huge crowd on all three days.

He thanked Mr. John for arranging the fixture, and the Devonshire team for accepting defeat "in the manner long expected of English gentlemen".

The new ground at Chapel Hill Cross had proved itself to be a perfect venue for cricket, and he hoped that membership of the club would grow, as more and more people chose to come to live in Torquay.

He saved a special thanks for Mr. Hearder who had provided the accommodation for the Eleven, and thanked the umpires, the scorers, and the many local people who had carried out minor roles in seeing that the match ran smoothly.

Finally, he promised to improve the playing surface, and said that he had begun by putting money aside to buy horse boots to allow the pitch to be rolled before next season began.

His speech received generous applause from the whole gathering.

Mr. Nicholas Felix replied on behalf of the Eleven, whilst Old Clarke stood erect and motionless, in black, behind him.

Mr. Felix thanked the club for the welcome extended to his team, and hoped that it would invite them again next year.

The catering had been superb, and the accommodation, overlooking the harbour, would stay in his mind forever.

It was a pity the match had ended earlier than expected, but at least the sheep would have an early dinner tonight!

Before closing, he asked all members of the Eleven to step forward and to give a special rendering of a song which he said had been written by "Our captain, William".

I glanced at Clarke, but that usual slightly quizzical expression remained totally unmoved.

It was the first time I had heard the song, but all the other players joined in.

It was sung to the tune of "Rule Britannia" and even I began to join in its chorus.

"Then success to cricket / 'tis a noble game / it's patronised by royalty, and men of wealth and fame!"

The crowd loved it, and was joining in too before the end.

Just as the song was ending, I saw the Eleven's "Diligence" coach coming through the bottom gate, and, within moments, the coachman had pulled it up behind us.

No one was paying it much attention as one of the elderly ladies stepped forward and handed a box to Mr. Cary. He put it on a table beside him, and then asked each of the Eleven to step forward.

As they did so, he shook hands and handed each of them an earthenware stirrup cup, decorated with the letters "TCC – 1853" as a memento of their visit.

Again, the crowd applauded the gesture, and even Old Clarke nodded his thanks.

It had been a perfect ending to a wonderful three days, and, one by one, the players waved as they climbed up into the coach.

I had a brief chance to shake Joe's hand before he joined them, and, at the coachman's call, the horses turned and headed off towards the gate.

At least a dozen arms were still waving from the windows as the coach turned again and headed for the station.

I looked around for Mr. John, but he had gone back into the pavilion with the Devonshire players.

Williams was sitting on the pavilion steps, chatting to two friends.

I hoped that he would, one day, be the umpire this club deserved, and felt just slightly envious that he could spend his summers here, on this meadow, which had become such a perfect little cricket ground.

It was time to go now, so I picked up my box and my bag and made my way slowly through the crowd to the top gate.

Chapel Hill and the railway station were ahead of me, but as I passed under the oak tree by the gate, I looked back for one last time on a little ground which had provided me with memories that would last me a lifetime.

Just as I did so, my eyes began to flicker, and I felt a sharp pain in my neck.

Had I fallen? I didn't know, but for some reason I was seated now, and my vision was blurred.

I took a deep breath, and cleared my eyes.

The little thatched pavilion was gone, and where was the oak tree at the top end? Everything had changed in an instant!

As I sat up, I ached all over, and the man in front of me turned round in his deckchair and grinned. He nudged his wife, and she looked at me and smiled.

Slowly, I woke up to the world around me, and it seemed dull compared to the one I had just left.

I had been dreaming in technicolour, and had woken up in a black and white world.

It was time to go home now, and write my match report... or was it?

As I got up, I felt, strangely fulfilled. It was if I had just completed a wonderful day of cricket, not just woken from a long sleep in a deckchair!

I stood up, propped up my chair against the fence, and made my way out on to Barton Road.

As I reached Torre School, I thought I saw a man dressed in black on the other side of the road.

He seemed to look over at me and to tip his top hat!

But, before I had the chance to see if he had chalk on his arm, he was gone.

Jenny was waiting for me when I got home, and made us a cup of tea.

"So! Did anything interesting happen at the cricket?" she asked.

"Yes! I suppose it did," I replied.

CHAPTER SIXTEEN

As the days passed, I realised that during my dream I had met a lot of wonderful people, and, in many cases, had warmed to them.

Did Joe play in the next match as he had hoped?

Did Old Clarke retain his players despite the call of the United England Eleven?

Did Mr. John inherit Lupton House, and what happened to Charlotte and the children?

After a while I needed to know, so spent some months researching at my desk.

Here is what I managed to find out:

Joe Guy… two days after we shook hands, Clarke picked Joe to play at Islington, and he top scored in the match with 27. History doesn't record whether he bought a bat from Eleanor Page, or even if he "nuzzled her neck" to do so!

He played one more year for the All England Eleven before retiring to become an inn keeper in his native Nottingham.

William Clarke… his All England Eleven continued to tour the country until the 1870s, but, sadly, outlived its founder.

The Cricket Ground at Cricketfield Road as it is today.

Old Clarke died just three years after I had chalked him, but, in a final act of defiance, he took a wicket with the last ball he ever bowled!

The Hon. John Yarde-Buller... who befriended me that day at Teignbridge, died young at just forty-three.

He never inherited the title of Baron Churston from his father, who outlived him by four years. In his place, little John, whom I had met at Churston Court, became the Second Baron Churston.

Mr. John resigned as the secretary of Teignbridge Cricket Club after 1854, but continued on the club's committee for a further year. He remained as a player until 1858.

Old Tom Box… that great wicket-keeper, with whom I had enjoyed so many chats in the marquee, played for the All England Eleven for another two years.

After retiring from cricket, he found employment in several trades, but never with much success.

Eventually, he became the attendant and ground keeper at Prince's Ground in Chelsea, London.

He died at the ground in 1876, on the last day of the match between Middlesex and Nottinghamshire, just as he was altering the score on the scoreboard.

"Topper" Hillyer… who took eighteen wickets in the match at Chapel Hill Cross, succumbed to his gout, and never played another season for the Eleven.

After retirement, he was the victim of rheumatism, and never returned to fitness before his death in 1861 at the age of forty-seven.

George Parr… who hit a ball right over the pavilion at Chapel Hill Cross, and showed us how to hold eight chicken drumsticks in both hands, became the leading professional batsman in England.

He captained Nottinghamshire, and led the very first England overseas cricket tour, to North America in 1859. Four years later, he captained a tour to Australia.

"Cris" Tinley… one of the three "given men" to assist the 22 of Devonshire during the match at Chapel Hill Cross, had a poor game that day.

Within twelve months, he had given up fast round-arm bowling, and taught himself to bowl under-arm lobs.

He was so successful that he became one of the first great lob bowlers, and, in 1863, was chosen to tour Australia under George Parr.

The seventeen-year-old Hon. Mark Rolle, who was the undisputed favourite of the young ladies under the oak tree, resisted their charms and, in 1860, married Lady Gertrude Jane Douglas.

In the following year, he was made Barnstaple's High Steward, and, in 1864, became Sheriff of Devon.

Julius Caesar, who top scored in the match at Chapel Hill Cross, accompanied his friend, George Parr, on the tours to North America and Australia.

"Julie" continued to play some fine innings for Surrey before succumbing to gout, and an early retirement. He died at the Railway Tavern in Godalming, aged just forty-seven.

Just weeks after the match at Chapel Hill Cross, the Crimean War began, and continued for over two years. Sadly, I was unable to find out whether my dear friend, Captain Budd, became involved in the war, and, if so, whether he survived it.

Finally, I traced young Parker, who helped around the ground, and came on as a substitute for Topper Hillyer when the All England Eleven needed him.

Jim became the editor of two Torquay newspapers, a very good local cricketer, and has remained an ageless campaigner for Chapel Hill Cross ever since.

This book is printed on paper from sustainable sources managed under the Forest Stewardship Council (FSC) scheme.

It has been printed in the UK to reduce transportation miles and their impact upon the environment.

For every new title that Matador publishes, we plant a tree to offset CO_2, partnering with the More Trees scheme.

For more about how Matador offsets its environmental impact, see www.troubador.co.uk/about/